V O I C E S *of*
N O R T H   A N D   S O U T H
O C K E

CW01095162

To Bill
with best wishes
from
Olive Pyke
May 2014

VOICES *of*
NORTH AND SOUTH
OCKENDON

CECILIA PYKE

The
History
Press

First published 2014

The History Press
The Mill, Brimscombe Port
Stroud, Gloucestershire, GL5 2QG
www.thehistorypress.co.uk

British Library Cataloguing in Publication Data.
A catalogue record for this book is available from the British Library.

ISBN 978 0 7524 9918 5

Typesetting and origination by The History Press
Printed in Great Britain

CONTENTS

ACKNOWLEDGEMENTS

I should like to thank everybody who helped me with the compilation of this book. Without your knowledge of the area, help in finding contacts, photographs and giving so generously of your time, it would never have been accomplished. Special thanks must go to John Litton, who tirelessly rummaged through his archives to find what I needed, to Pam Bonnett for introducing me to so many North Ockendon people, to Geoff Jones for his vast input and Jan Jones for supplying so many photographs.

I've loved getting to know you all, so please forgive any mistakes I might have made, and take my good wishes for the future.

I've based, where possible, all historical facts on the *Victoria History of the County of Essex* and every effort has been made to trace the origins of photographs, with acknowledgements where appropriate.

INTRODUCTION

The road that passes through the villages of South and North Ockendon was established in the Middle Ages as the route between Grays and Brentwood. Little has changed, although the area within the south-west of South Ockendon has seen its road network altered due to building works.

Although Belhus mansion was in the postal district of Aveley, part of its grounds were in South Ockendon, so it would be appropriate to mention a little of its history. The London County Council and Essex County Council bought much of the Belhus estate and surrounding farmland in the 1930s. The Hon. J.D. Fitzgerald lived in the mansion for a short time but, during the Second World War, the army took over the house and park. When they left, the house fell into disrepair and then there was a fire, so it was demolished in 1957. All that is left of its existence is the old stench pipe which is near the Long Pond, but other artefacts can be found in various museums.

After the war, Essex County Council bought a considerable amount of the remaining land for the purpose of building a housing estate and, in the late 1950s, work began to create housing mainly for the overspill from London. We now have the well-established Belhus estate, which is separated by Belhus Park from the Kennington estate, which is in Aveley.

South Ockendon is an ancient parish. It was a community long before the Norman invasion and had its own church by 1085, with a recorded population of just sixty-six people. The place name Ockendon is said to originate from 'Woccaduna' (spelt various ways,) which is derived from the name of the Saxon chief, Wocca.

South Ockendon and a little of North Ockendon come under the auspices of Thurrock, while the remainder of North Ockendon is part of the London Borough of Havering. The villages have distinctly different characters. North Ockendon remains sleepy and composed whilst South Ockendon, although still retaining its central village charm, is more overt and densely populated.

In 1849 Richard Benyon de Beauvoir bought the manor of South Ockendon and its surroundings, and his heirs (also Richard Benyons) continued to be benefactors to both South and North Ockendon, with the schools and churches being the main recipients of their largesse.

In 1863 Richard Benyon built a new National School in West Road, opposite the village green. At that time truancy was a problem during harvesting season, as children were expected to help with pea picking and bird scaring. He also built the teacher's house in 1896 and, in 1957, the school was taken over by the Education Committee and renamed Benyon School for Juniors and Infants.

The early 1900s saw the foundations laid of what was to become a big employer of local people in South Ockendon – the South Ockendon Hospital. Around the same time, Little Mollands farm was sold to West Ham Borough Council for use as a farm colony, where unemployed men could work for their dole money. German prisoners of war were housed there during the First World War and, in 1932, it became a colony for those in need of psychiatric care. It was established as the South Ockendon Hospital in 1948 and took many affected people under its wing. For many years it provided vital help for those unable to take care of themselves but, when attitudes towards mental health changed, it gradually moved its residents into the communities and finally closed its doors in 1994.

The hospital was destroyed and in its place Brandon Groves, a privately owned housing estate, was established. Naming the roads after those of the hospital wards ensures that the past is not forgotten. A small memorial garden was established on the site and the hospital's old entertainment hall remains within Brandon Groves, where it still functions as a community centre.

North Ockendon has been a mainly arable farming community for centuries, and remains largely undisturbed. In 1066 it had a recorded population of just seventeen. Modernisation has changed some aspects with Baldwin's, the oldest recorded farm in the area, ceasing to function as such, and some other farms having been integrated into larger units. There is no longer a village blacksmith; Puddledock Farm is now a popular haunt with fishermen and a few barns have been converted into homes.

St Mary's Church of England School in Church Lane originated in 1842 when Richard Benyon de Beauvoir built a school and teacher's house by subscription. He was then Lord of the Manor. The school was rebuilt by his successor – also named Richard Benyon – in 1902, when eighty children attended. It was damaged by bombs in late 1944 and, by 1947, when attendance had been reduced to thirty pupils, the council suggested it should be closed. It remained open nonetheless but finally closed its doors in 1980.

To pass through North Ockendon today is almost to step back in time, even with the busy M25 passing through it. The church is still very popular, with attendees from Upminster swelling the congregation.

Both North and South Ockendon have a rich history, far more than can be mentioned in this book, with some of the old buildings still standing. The Royal Oak public house is thought to be the oldest, apart from the churches, and we mustn't forget Little Belhus House and Quince Tree Cottage. Sadly, the windmills no longer exist. The names of such dignitaries as Poyntz, Saltonstall, Capability Brown, William Coys, Littlejohn, and more recently Benyon, trip lightly from the lips of locals.

This book deals mainly with social history, and within its pages you will meet some of its residents – real people who remember the old times and repeat the stories told by those who came before them. They are the voices of the Ockendons, and it was my pleasure to record their stories.

One

EARLY LIFE AND SCHOOLDAYS

The Street

The village school in South Ockendon stood in The Street, the original name of West Road. The doctor's house, named Pear Tree, was virtually next door and during my childhood Dr McFarlane lived there. The school bell would be rung by the caretaker every morning to tell us not to be late, but in my grandmother's time there, the oldest girls did the ringing.

Ann Staff

Farmer Hoare

My family moved to South Ockendon in about November 1951 – our address was Daiglen Drive, Belhus Park, South Ockendon near Romford, Essex, and at that time we were part of the village.

Farmer Hoare had the farm on which Little Belhus House stands and there were barns near the house. There was a little farm labourer's cottage nearby and the Carsons lived there with their daughter, Sylvie. Mr Carson worked for the Ham River Grit Company – he was the nightwatchman and had a lovely sheepdog. I know all this because I was their paper boy. The farm used to run along the Ham River site and there were no factories in the area then.

Denis Powell

School Dinners

I first went to school in the 'huts' near Dilkes Park, which were used as an overspill from local schools they were building. In the summer we'd take our tables outside and have lessons sitting in front of the Nissen huts in the sunshine. Later I went to Shaw in Daiglen Drive and I remember there was another school in the area called Somers Heath. There was the Catholic school called Holy Cross, and there was Culverhouse, which was a secondary school where boys and girls were educated separately. I think they eventually pulled the schools down and built houses on the site.

We had wonderful school dinners in those days with home-made pies, etc. I think the food was cooked at Culverhouse and brought over to our school – it was absolutely lovely. Back then they used the cane and I was the only boy in my class who'd not been caned in primary school. Although when I was caned in senior school, it was for something I'd not done.

My favourite sweets were Refreshers and I also liked Bazooka bubble gum because I could collect the cards in the packets. I was given pocket money and saved it to buy premium bonds, but because I was too young to have them in my name, they were put in the name of my mother. I forgot all about them and when she died I didn't bother to cash them in, so saving them didn't do me much good. That was fifty years ago and I still have them in a box somewhere.

Adrian Inglefield

The Miss Wards

I went to North Ockendon School when I was about five and it was run by two Miss Wards – one taught and one acted as housekeeper. We used to deliver their groceries and sometimes Dad would slip half a bottle of whiskey into their basket. Miss Cole used to teach there as well. We had little gardens at the back of the school where we grew vegetables, rhubarb and suchlike. When I was eleven I went on to Gaynes in Upminster.

I was in the Scouts and during the week we met in the Reading Room – there were about thirty of us and the group used to go camping in Somerset. I played the usual sports at school: football, rounders and stool-board. We'd keep all the gear in the rectory, where the Revd Lister was living at the time. He was also rector to The Colony and several of the inmates used to come up to do some sweeping and dusting. He was rector at Stifford too, where they had a borstal. Our church was St Mary Magdalene and he used to get the borstal boys

St Mary Magdalene Church School.

North Ockendon Rectory, 1962.

to come to Sunday service. One Sunday they burgled the Old White Horse on their way.

The Reading Room played a large part in our lives back then – it was organised by the church but given to the village by Benyon. The Benyons were rich and benefactors to North Ockendon. Years later, my wife and I were to hold our wedding reception there. I was in the church choir and also used to pump the organ. Boys will be boys, so I'd read a comic in between times and received many a thump from Miss Cole. The vicarage has since been sold.

Peter Coe

Swimming Pool

I came to live in South Ockendon in 1972, when I was four years old. My first school was Mardyke primary, which was in Cruick Avenue. I can remember the names of some of the teachers: Mrs Kirby and Mrs Howels, among others. But my strongest memory is of the swimming pool, as it was unusual for a school to have one in those days and it was where I learnt to swim. The children would be given little stripes as they became able to do more lengths. Mr Osborne was my form teacher and I'm not sure why, but the school was knocked down at some point and houses were built on the site.

As a senior, I went to Culverhouse until my third year and remember that Mrs Levy and Mrs Thomas both taught science. Shortly after, I was transferred to a school in Aveley where Pat Rice taught geography. He later became a councillor.

Dacre Centre for the handicapped was on the opposite side of the road to the school and we used to chat with the residents when we came out of lessons.

Maria Proctor

Barretts

I started school at Barretts in South Ockendon and went on to attend South Ockendon Court School, where we wore blue uniforms. Another school was Lennards, where they wore green, and the pupils of Culverhouse wore brown.

Margaret Abboyi

St Thomas's, Grays

As there was no Catholic school in South Ockendon when we came to live here, from the age of five I'd walk across the fields from Araglen Avenue to Ford Place. I'd get on the bus to Grays, where I went to St Thomas's. When I was eleven I went to South Ockendon Court School.

Lessons for the first Catholic school in South Ockendon, which was called Holy Cross, were held in the church hall until the purpose-built school was ready – this was in the 1950s. It was run by Sister Dominic and Joe Graham. Mr Graham, who was a brilliant teacher, went on to become headmaster of St Peter's in Dagenham.

Roz Hadley

Paddy the Park-keeper

Dilkes Park was where we children liked playing. There was a park-keeper in those days – his name was Paddy, so we knew him as Paddy the Park-keeper. He kept his tools in his shed and we liked to go in with him to chat – he was a lovely man and kind to us children. The park was always immaculate and there was a big paddling area made of stone so in the summer he'd fill it up for us so we could paddle. Sometimes he'd be sitting outside the shed in a deckchair and we'd sit on the grass chatting to him on the way home from school.

Maria Proctor

Earning Pocket Money

While I was at school I did several jobs. I worked for Casts the bakers on a Saturday. Pedalling their big old three-wheeler bike, I'd go down to Bulphan then to West Horndon with bread and rolls, then go over to the firm that did metal piping. After that I'd take two loads to The Colony and make another two trips to the army camp in Buckles Lane. I'd also work during the evenings and school holidays for Young's the grocers, delivering groceries for them on their old trade bike. When I came out of school during the week I did a paper round at night time. I'd start off by the railway station, go right round to North Ockendon then do part of North Road on a bike. It was fairly easy to get a little job back then, although we earned peanuts really and used to spend the money on sweets.

Eric Jiggens

South Ockendon village scene, around the 1930s.

Clean Shoes

When I was four I started school at Benyon's in South Ockendon and had to walk across the fields to get there. The Benyon family owned quite a lot of land in the area at that time. The headmaster was very strict about his pupils' shoes being clean which would be a problem for us on wet days, but Dad cleaned our shoes every night. Luckily, Grandmother Scott lived in South Ockendon so I went to her for my midday meal; otherwise I'd have taken sandwiches. The headmaster's house was near the school and sometimes we'd help with the gardening. He had a walled garden which was full of roses and other lovely flowers. When I was eleven I transferred to Gaynes School in Upminster and transport was laid on, but I still had to walk to South Ockendon to get the school coach.

Joy Scott

The Registrar

I first started school at Oglethorpe as at the time the only Catholic school I could have attended was St Thomas's in Grays, but my parents thought it too far for me to travel. My father was registrar for marriages in Holy Cross on the Belhus estate. Holy Cross School was in Daiglen Drive.

Denis Powell

Benyon Primary School, 2013.

Garage on the A127

I was born in 1917 and spent my childhood in Basildon, which was still a lovely little village in those days. It had, and indeed still has, a beautiful church. My father had been brought up with cars and had worked for the White Steam Company. He was a mechanic and when horse-drawn vehicles were replaced, part of his job was to go round to the big houses to teach the grooms how to drive.

We came to Basildon from Hampstead and lived in a bungalow next door to the garage we had on the A127. At that time the road was a single carriageway but it was gradually widened and extended until, on 25 March 1925, it was officially opened by Prince Henry, who later became Duke of Gloucester. We had the first garage on the A127 from London to Southend and sold teas to customers from the front room of the bungalow. Unfortunately it was flooded in the 1950s so the family went to live in Billericay.

I went to a junior school in Basildon but later travelled to Brentwood County High School on a bus which was specially laid on for us. My elder brother was away at school – he was a boarder – while my little brother and my future husband went to school together in Grays. They were scholarship boys at the John Henry Burrows School at the top of Hathaway Road.

Evelyn Cressey

Hornchurch Baths

I went to the Barretts school and loved it. My teacher lived at the Upminster end of Hornchurch and we used to cycle over there at the weekend. We were ten or eleven at that time – imagine that – we had an awful lot of freedom in those days. We'd cycle to Hornchurch baths, and in the summer we went to Dagenham open-air swimming pool. Nothing was given to us – we had to work for our pocket money by washing up at night and cleaning our bedrooms on Saturdays. The boys also helped Dad if he needed it.

Carole Jones

Two

NEWCOMERS

Belhus Park

My parents were newcomers to South Ockendon and I was born in Daiglen Drive in 1953 but I left the Ockendon area in 1964, so my memories are of my early years.

I recall the fun I had in Belhus Park, where I used to play in those days. The park was in Garron Lane and there was a cattle grid at the entrance, as cows were grazing on the field where the golf course now stands.

There was a concrete strip in the park which was laid in sections, each strip being about five foot in length and twelve foot wide. My Dad taught me to ride my bicycle on it. We used to go for bike rides regularly and would sometimes pass the railway station with its coal depot and then go on into North Ockendon. We'd ride all over the place – Stifford, Grays and Purfleet, etc.

Sometimes we'd catch the train from South Ockendon to Grays and thence to Southend. They did a special trip on Saturdays and the train was always packed.

We'd take the bus into Grays and go to the cinema quite regularly. There were four picture houses – the Ritz, the Regal, the State and the Eagle. By the time we'd sat through the 'A' film, the 'B' film, trailers, adverts and the Pathé News, the trip would have taken half a day. The cinemas were well supported back then with a smart commissionaire on the door, usherettes and plush seating, etc.

I can remember the time when the housing estate which separates Daiglen Drive from Derwent Parade wasn't there. The site was just a big field with some trees on it where lorries parked, and you could see right through to Derwent Parade shops.

A fair used to come to South Ockendon twice a year and they'd use the field to set up their rides and stalls, etc. I also remember the field being used for a fight between some mods and rockers – quite a serious one involving a good few hundred chaps.

The Eastern National Bus used to go from Tilbury Riverside through Grays and South Ockendon village and on to Brentwood. A Green Line bus ran from Grays along the A13 to Aldgate East. The 723A began at Rainham, down through Sandy Lane, through the village, down Foyle Drive, along Daiglen Drive then on to Grays. The 371 went from Grays, through South and North Ockendon and out to Brentwood.

Adrian Inglefield

No Shops

There were no shops when we moved to South Ockendon in 1950, so we had to walk through Foyle Drive to Garron Lane, but it was a bit of a hike as I was only five years old. The estate is nothing like it was then. There were open spaces with lots of trees for us to climb, so we had plenty of room to play. The present open space near Lidl was full of trees then. Apart from that the whole area was a building site, so we children were able to get into plenty of mischief. There were no parks with swings.

When I reached fourteen I got a Saturday job so my brothers had to do a little more to help out than they had been doing.

Carole Jones

Mr Watts

My parents moved into Araglen Avenue in South Ockendon on 2 May 1950 so I've lived around here for a long time. The whole area, which is now a housing estate, was all trees then. As children, we'd walk to Belhus Park where Mr Watts, the farmer, kept his cows. We'd push them aside when they got in our way – he seemed to have cows roaming around the place in those days. What we know as Belhus Park was all part of the grounds surrounding the Belhus mansion with a public right of way from Humber Avenue into the Kennington estate. We'd get our milk from Mr Watts and he used to bring us vegetables from his farm. When he died his sons ran the farm and they continued to bring the milk.

None of the shops that exist on the estate were built then – we'd have to go into South Ockendon village for our shopping, or further afield to Grays. I can

Derwent Parade, around 1970.

remember the buildings we called the Nissen hut schools in Fayemore Gardens, just by Dilkes Wood, and later the prefabs.

There was a timber yard in South Road where we'd buy wood for the fire.

My mother had been a nursing sister in Rampton Mental Hospital, so she worked in the South Ockendon one for some time too. I worked there as well, as did many of the people round here. Some of the patients were pretty bad but there was a good atmosphere amongst the staff. We all had distinctive uniforms with a sister wearing navy blue, a state enrolled nurse wearing dark green while the auxiliaries wore white.

Later I went to work for Fords in Arisdale Avenue and really enjoyed my time there.

Roz Hadley

The Royal Oak, 2013.

Abattoir

Our family moved to Ockendon and lived in Easington Way on the Belhus estate and it's where I was born. The house was opposite the Catholic church and we were near the shops and library. The first of the housing estates built by the London County Council after the war was Dagenham, followed by Harold Hill, and then South Ockendon. They were all built to the same design.

I remember there was a row of prefabs in Foxglove in South Ockendon village, but later most of these were replaced by a different type of prefabricated house which was built of slabs. They too have since been replaced as they weren't very nice.

There were two estates in the area, with Belhus being built as extra housing for South Ockendon, and Kennington, which provided more housing for Aveley village. They were separated by Belhus Park and again they're both of the same design.

My father was a carpenter/joiner and during the '60s he worked on the site of the abattoir. The size of the abattoir was gradually being reduced, with private housing being built in its place and Dad worked on the roofing. The abattoir was still operating and Dad said he never got used to the awful sound of the pigs shrieking as they were shepherded in for slaughter.

Eventually it closed with more houses being built on the remaining area. Dad was an atheist and not fanciful but said that every now and again there'd be an incident that shocked him – but he wouldn't talk about it. Security guards with dogs were employed at night and the dogs would howl and bark as if they were petrified of something.

Sometimes Dad would go into work very early in the morning to scour the site for evidence of something sinister, but found nothing untoward; although it got to the point where the usual dogs wouldn't enter the site, so new dogs had to be brought in. These acted in the same way and even turned on their normal handlers, necessitating a constant change of guards.

Some years later, I did some babysitting for a family who moved into one of the houses built on the abattoir site, but nothing peculiar happened.

There wasn't a bus going to South Ockendon station from where I lived and it would have taken me twenty minutes to walk there, so it was easier to get on a bus at the end of our road which went to Rainham station, and a group of us travelled together. There were factories along the road from South Ockendon station to home which was another reason that put me off walking along there, but I understand it's on a bus route now.

When we were children there were always stories going around about the sighting of ghosts around the cemetery and The Royal Oak and I heard somewhere that South Ockendon is the most haunted village in Essex; it's alleged there have been many eerie sightings along the main road to Brentwood but I can't say I've seen anything myself.

In the '70s, I used to help out at the stables near Belhus Park. It was only a small family concern which was run by a man who had three daughters. They had about three horses each and he kept them all. The stables only opened at weekends and some of us local girls used to help by taking people for rides in Belhus Park, so we were able to get our own rides for nothing. The father was a real horseman himself who taught us how to jump etc. He used to take his horses to graze on the marshes on Sunday and bring them back to Belhus on Friday afternoon.

We were aware of the mental hospital in South Ockendon because Mum, who was not a drama queen, always used to say 'if you hear the siren going, it means a patient has escaped from the hospital, so you need to come home'.

Margaret Abboyi

Three

THE SECOND WORLD WAR

Elsan Toilet

We lived at the far end of the village, very near the Buckles Lane army camp, which played its part with great gusto by trying to shoot down the enemy planes which came over us primarily to get to London. The guns there were known as heavy ack-ack and our home shook with each salvo. Not only did the German planes try to bomb Hornchurch Aerodrome; they tried to bomb the camp one night and succeeded in dropping a fairly small bomb on the gun emplacements, killing two or three ATS girls who were helping to man them. I used to hear the guns start up in the distance and get closer and louder until the siren went off, and then off would go the camp's guns.

English and German planes had different sounding engines and I knew the difference but my mother didn't, so I used to tell her what was overhead at the time.

I remember one night standing in the back garden with my mother, watching London burning during the Blitz. We saw the tops of flames above the trees; the sky was red.

The morning after a raid, children would collect up shrapnel and keep it to look at and compare. Later on in the war the V1s (doodle-bugs) came about. We used to stand and watch them come overhead towards London with the flames coming from the back. We hoped they wouldn't shut off because when they did, the thing would plummet to earth with a whooshing sound and explode. One landed on some waste ground in the centre of the village and badly damaged some council houses opposite. My aunt had her doors and windows blown in. A while later the V2 rocket came into existence. These were completely silent until they exploded on impact, which was utterly frightening as you didn't

High Street, South Ockendon, around the 1900s.

know they were coming. Sitting at piano practise one evening, our light went out. I knew something was happening and was told to crouch under the piano keyboard, whereupon an almighty bang occurred but nothing visible. In the morning I was sent to the village proper to see what had happened. A rocket had landed in exactly the same hole as that made previously by the doodle-bug. This rocket had finished off the damaged houses and caused two fatalities. My aunt's doors and windows had been blown out again.

I attended the village school where my forebears had gone and of course, because of the war, we spent much time in the brick-built air-raid shelters. We sat in virtual darkness on wooden forms often wearing our gas masks for practise, which was uncomfortable and they steamed up. The toilet, an Elsan, was behind a curtain and it was an embarrassment to use it as every sound carried, which made us giggle. We had to swallow cod liver oil and malt every morning before we left for school and orange juice mixed with water.

Ann Staff

Fast Asleep

The army used the area we now know as Belhus Park to store their equipment during the war. Several regiments were billeted in the mansion before they were posted abroad. The army also took over Ford Place which they used as offices –

Churchill used to go there. They used Ford Place as an army hospital after the war. There's a massive walled garden at the back of the house.

The council put big concrete blocks and empty oil containers on the recreation ground so German planes couldn't land, and we made our own fun by jumping around them and running about letting off steam, as boys do.

At one time we were all in the shelter when a bomb dropped nearby. Mum and my brothers and sisters rushed back to the house to get out of the way and they realised I wasn't with them. Mum didn't know if I was dead or alive but when they thought to search the shelter, I was inside, fast asleep. I didn't hear the bombs going off.

Eric Jiggens

Tragedy

I had a brother who was three years older than me but he was killed while flying in Egypt during the war. I'd been called up myself and was in the shop waiting to go to Cardington when my parents received a telegram to say he'd been killed. It was a terrible day for our family, but I had to leave immediately to join the air force.

Peter Coe

Rationing

I was born in the early 1900s and had four brothers and three sisters. I moved to South Ockendon in the 1970s and loved being able to see trees and open spaces as I was born in the East End and spent the war years there. If the siren sounded when I was at work in the laundry shop in the Mile End Road, we used to go into the cellar of the shop next door. They were dreadful times and we were bombed out on several occasions. People would go to 'centres' where they gave us things so we could carry on – they were lovely people.

My husband worked in the foundry so we'd use their shelter at night because it was very deep. We'd take our bedclothes and sleep down there, although my husband did fire-watching at night. He died from lung cancer, which they reckon was brought about by the fumes from the foundry.

Food was rationed, of course, although we kept chickens so were able to have some meat, and my uncle had rabbits that we ate at weddings and Christmas. We were only allowed a couple of ounces of meat per week by the government, although the official line was it could cost no more than 1s 2d.

Most of our food was imported – it had to come in on merchant ships which were liable to attack from U-boats. The amount of food we were allowed seem to change all the time, I suppose depending on what the government could get hold of. We only had one egg each a week on ration. Our family had a few more as we got them from our chickens but they didn't go far as there were a lot of us. Then there was that egg powder – we could have a packet each every four weeks, and we had 'points' for tinned food.

I seem to remember that bacon, sugar and butter were the first to be rationed. They began to ration clothing later on but, like everything else, what you were allowed changed all the time, and I think clothes rationing didn't end until 1949.

Amy (Dolly) Manning

Ministry of Works

A doodle-bug and a rocket dropped in South Ockendon, doing quite a bit of damage. Since my grandmother and uncles lived there I visited quite often. During the latter part of the war I was working in the garage so experienced the doodle-bugs etc. After an incident the Ministry of Works used to come round in big articulated lorries, carrying living accommodation and cooking facilities. They'd bring workmen to do emergency repairs – they'd park up on the village green and mend windows and put roofs back on, etc.

John Litton

Sound Barrier

Hall Farm was one of a few farms permitted to grow outdoor tomatoes during the war, and had several acres of plants produced from a nursery in Victoria Road, Romford. Although Messrs Gunary had their own sales stand in Covent Garden they were not allowed to sell them, as sales were restricted to one trade-stand. This meant they had to pay commission on sales of their own produce. Although it was kept pretty quiet, a plot was hatched for one of the lorry drivers, Mr Byford, to 'accidentally' back his lorry into the stack of tomato boxes on the rival stand, knock them down and then apologise profusely for the accident. Mr Byford was not one to apologise to anyone so I assume he had been adequately compensated to do this by all the other tomato growers as well.

Following the bombs falling on North Ockendon Hall, the Royal Navy were very interested in what type of 'mines' they were, although later it was confirmed that they were two of the largest bombs dropped on Britain. The day after the bombs fell, a naval officer arrived at the school in Church Lane and asked that we children collect as many fragments as we could find and eventually quite a pile was made in the playground. Most of the boys had collected many pieces of shrapnel, shellcaps, pieces of bombs and rockets etc., and I retained, and still have, a couple of pieces of the bombs that fell near North Ockendon Hall. I can still recall the night they fell. It was blowing a gale and raining hard, when all the ceilings of our house in Church Lane fell. All the doors were blown open and my mother just sat and cried because my father was out with the Auxiliary Fire Service and she didn't know where he was. The ceiling had fallen on my little sister's bed but it didn't wake her. She finally woke up amongst the panic and, not knowing what had happened, she calmly got out of bed, walked round it, and got back in on the other side.

There was an anti-aircraft gun emplacement on land still owned by the Ministry of Defence on top of the hill, which can be reached by the footpath that runs from the end of the garden of White Post Farm, up to the trig point on top of the hill. As you reach the end of the field, on the right near the rear boundary of the nursing home, you can still see the concrete gun sites. An army camp was built in Fen Lane, opposite to Corner Farm cottages, to house the troops that served the guns. One fine morning, looking east from a bedroom window, we saw vapour trails rising from the launch of V2 rockets in Holland. My father said it would take about six minutes before they arrived and we'd hear a bang. Often we'd hear a double bang as a rocket passed overhead and we always assumed this was from the engine being reignited. It wasn't until after the war, when research into planes breaking the sound barrier began, that we realised what we'd heard had indeed been the sound barrier being broken by the rockets.

I can also remember the first night of the V1 doodle-bug attacks. Our neighbour – Ernie Bennett – who was an elderly horseman on Hall Farm and a fire-watcher, knocked on our door to tell us a German plane which was on fire had crashed. Minutes later, there was a second knock to say another plane was on fire and had crashed. When it got to number ten or so, we realised that perhaps things were not as they appeared. It was confirmed on the news next day that the flying-bomb era had started.

The V1s came over during the day as well as at night and one flew over Church Lane from the south-east one evening. It passed very low over our house and the engine cut out. This usually resulted in it diving straight into the ground and exploding on impact. We threw ourselves onto the ground, waiting for the explosion, but fortunately for us it just glided on and fell behind the

Windmill at South Ockendon, 1700s. (Courtesy of Brian Evans)

Thatched House public house on the junction of Pike Lane and St Mary's Lane. I think the crater is still visible in the same way as the rocket crater in Fen Lane, i.e. a ring of bushes with a pond/hollow in the centre.

There was a searchlight placement at the end of the Old Bakery garden opposite Castle Cottages. I think the concrete base is still there. An anti-aircraft gun also ran on the railway line. We called it the 'pom pom' gun because of the sound it made but it was probably a Bofors, which was a rapid-fire gun.

A canister of incendiary bombs fell unopened into the ground in Pea Lane, on the right-hand side as you meet the first left-hand bend. A bomb disposal team dug for months trying to get it out, but the ground resembled quicksand and as fast as it was located it moved again. As far as I know it was never recovered and is probably still there.

There was a tragic collision of two B17 Flying Fortress planes. We were watching the return of squadrons of American planes one evening when one suddenly shot up, crashing into the underside of another and cutting its tail completely off. In the process the first plane lost a wing and both seemed to lazily spiral down. Although it probably happened quite quickly it seemed to take ages, with only one crew member managing to bail out from the severed tail. Both planes fell, with one exploding at what was known then as East Horndon (now West Horndon), while the remaining fifteen crew members lost their lives. Some wreckage from this crash is now, or was, in the Coalhouse Fort, East Tilbury.

Geoff Jones

Prisoner of War

When my future husband and his friend were eighteen, they were both stationed at Hornchurch Aerodrome. They joined the air force from school – they each sat the air force entrance exam for a practice and both passed – so they thought they might as well join up. My father had bought my brother a little Austin Seven and the boys were thinking about coming home, but the war broke out so they would have had to join up anyway. They were already in it, so to speak, and my husband trained as an aircraft fitter.

While he was at Hornchurch, a call came through to say one of our aircraft had landed on the French coast and a fitter was needed to do some work on the engine so the crew could fly the plane back. At that time they didn't know the Germans were advancing and all the crew, along with my husband, were taken prisoners of war. He spent the rest of the war in a prisoner-of-war camp although I can't remember which one. When it was over and the Americans were liberating the camps, my husband told me they walked halfway across Poland to meet them.

Evelyn Cressey

Tail End Charlie

I met my wife, Hilda, in Romford when I was in the air force, which I'd joined at the age of seventeen and a quarter. If you went into the air force you were normally taught a trade, with the exception of those who flew. I volunteered to fly in Lancaster bombers and any lad who flew was a volunteer. I'd only been in a car twice so the prospect of flying was a bit daunting but, at the same time, exciting. I found flying at 20,000 feet exhilarating and I loved it, despite the

Jim McGillivray as a young gunner at the rear turret, early 1940s.

fact I was the aircraft's rear gunner. I had to bail out by parachute one night at 18,500 feet. We managed to get back to England from Germany and I landed in a farmyard at about three o'clock in the morning. The farmer came out with a shotgun because he thought I was a German, but once he realised I wasn't the enemy, he made me a cup of tea and took me to the nearest aerodrome. I was flying again at nine o'clock the next day because it was the philosophy of the air force that you fly again as soon as possible. I flew for four years and was lucky to survive. Around 50,000 flyers from Bomber Command were killed but it took us seventy years to get a memorial for our service. There aren't many of us left now so I get asked to attend lots of events. I was a guest of honour at Westminster Abbey for the Battle of Britain celebrations amongst other things, and have met the Queen on more than one occasion.

I have three war medals: the 1939–45 Star, the France & Germany Star, the Victory Medal and the Caterpillar badge.

I'm a member of the Caterpillar Club, which is an informal association started in the early 1900s, which anybody who has bailed out from a disabled aircraft can join. The badge, which is traditionally worn on the tie, is made by Mappin & Webb, the queen's jeweller, and is about an inch long of pure gold with the name and rank of the owner engraved on the back. If an airman jumped from a burning plane his caterpillar will have two amethyst eyes. The caterpillar was chosen as a metaphor for the silk worm, i.e. the use of silk for the parachute, and for the caterpillar hanging by a silken thread when it falls from a tree. The motto of the Caterpillar Club is 'Life Depends on a Silken Thread'.

Jim McGillivray

Straw Everywhere

There was an army camp in Fen Lane but it wasn't there for long. Way back, before it became a golf course, there was a searchlight on Mill Meadow which linked up with the anti-aircraft battery in Buckles Lane, South Ockendon. There was a mock-up anti-aircraft gun in Fen Lane because it was on a high point, and even now there are some stone plinths in the hedges where you can see a battery point – they used to do lots of mock-ups during the war.

I still find bits of the German plane that came down in the field behind our house.

One of my uncles was in the North Ockendon Auxiliary Fire Service, based at White Post Farm, and when North Ockendon Hall was bombed in January 1944, he was one of the people who were called out. The Hall was hit by two high-explosive German bombs. My granddad had been thrashing up

North Ockendon Hall before it was bombed in 1944.

at the Hall about two weeks previously and there were two huge straw stacks which took most of the shock away from the house – there was straw all over the place. The bombs, which were called Max bombs, were the heaviest the Germans had, weighing two and a half tons and measuring over twelve feet long. The Hall had to be demolished but the walls that surrounded it can still be seen. The bombs also severely damaged the Old White Horse public house, two shops, the rectory, and about forty houses.

Steve White

Women's Land Army

Women's Land Army Girls were recruited as an option to joining the armed forces and replaced many of the men who were conscripted from the farms to fight in the war. There were many girls in the area and they came from all walks of life, from secretaries to domestic staff. Hall Farm had quite a few who came and went, but five of them remained on the farm for the duration of the war, and stayed until the late 1940s. The main hostel was a house called Hulmers, which still exists on Warley Street. It's just over the A127, on the left-hand side going towards Great Warley. It's a large white house which has a tall hedge in front of it, but originally it was quite open.

The girls cycled to the various farms, but soon some were billeted at the homes of farm workers. We had two of them billeted with us at No. 3, Church Lane. One was Joan Shakespeare, who before the war lived in Leigh-on-Sea, and had worked with her father and brother making artificial glass eyes. She lived with us for many years and always said my mother was like a mother to them both. She returned to her family firm after the war and kept in touch with us. Joan visited my mother regularly until Mum's death in 1999. She never married and spent a lot of her retired years sailing and travelling the world. The other girl was Gladys Harrington who had been a shorthand typist/secretary, and eventually became farm secretary to Cyril Gunary at Hall Farm.

Gladys corresponded regularly with a serving soldier named Arthur Griffiths, whom she had known before the war. He served with the 8th Army in North Africa, Italy, and Germany. They married after the war and, like Joan, she and Arthur kept in touch and visited my mother. Other girls I remember were Alice, Madeline and Daisy. Daisy married Jim Turner, who before the war had worked at Hall Farm before he too joined up.

Daisy and Jim lived in North Ockendon until their deaths, and had a son, David, who was at the village school at the same time as my children. When the

Group of Land Army Girls,
North Ockendon, 1942.

Joan Shakespeare, Land
Army Girl, 1942.

Land Army Girls first arrived I know it caused my father (who was then farm manager at Hall Farm) a great deal of frustration. It was quite a problem trying to teach town girls basic farm skills, as many didn't like their fingernails being chipped and full of soil. Getting some of the girls to bend down for small-hoeing and chopping out seedlings was near impossible. Mostly the girls were used for harvesting crops such as cutting asparagus, lettuce and cabbage, to digging parsnips, picking sprouts, beans, and bunching onions, etc. Some really didn't like the work, especially if it was raining, snowing, or just blowing a very cold gale. After a while things settled down and several of the most adaptable girls were retained and finished up really enjoying farm work. Many friendships developed between them and they integrated with the regular women workers and into village life very well, to such an extent that the main group remained working for many years.

Our friend, Joan Shakespeare, became a very competent horsewoman. At that time Hall Farm had around sixteen Suffolk Punch horses, and Joan was accepted by the horsemen. She did most of the work they did, from general land cultivation to carting produce from the fields in bushel boxes and bags to the packing shed. When the weather was very bad or in winter, the girls could be employed on several indoor jobs such as box mending, making up cardboard Filmer boxes for tomatoes, shelling runner beans for the seed, or scooping out marrows, again for the seed.

Geoff Jones

Barrage Balloon

I remember they had a barrage balloon at Stifford and the boys and girls from there came to a dance at The Colony. They had no transport so they tied the barrage balloon to the ground and borrowed the lorry which housed the winch. Unfortunately they had too much to drink and crashed the lorry on the way home, so were unable to raise the balloon until it was mended!

Peter Coe

Knitting Circle

During the war, Doris Stokes started a little knitting circle so we could make things to send to the soldiers. There were eight of us girls and for some reason she encouraged us to cycle round all the churches so we could sign their registers.

The knitting circle girls with their bicycles, around the 1940s.

I remember when the German fighter plane came down in the field at the back of our house. It had been shot down by an airman stationed at Hornchurch, who hitchhiked to North Ockendon after he'd landed. I remember him running into the field to see 'his plane' but the German pilot, who survived, had already blown the plane up and the last we saw of him was when he was being taken away by the police.

Dad was in the First Aid, so wasn't at home during a lot of the wartime, and I recall us children thinking it was great fun to watch the dogfights which took place over our area.

Convoys used to come through North Road on their way to the docks and the despatch riders, who always went ahead, got into the habit of telling Mum a convoy was on its way so she could make the soldiers a cup of tea.

We used to go to dances at Warley Barracks. Five or six of us girls would go there by bus and have a jolly good time dancing with the soldiers to the music played by the Essex Regimental Band. We always shared a taxi home.

Gwen Bishop

Phosphorus and Airguns

During the war my father was in the Home Guard. They had some early Lee Enfield rifles and did their practising down at Mill Meadow.

We had quite a few raids round here and one night a lot of incendiary bombs fell alongside the railway line out at the back. The fields had been ploughed, making it easier for us to see them, and it had been raining. We used to go down there with blocks of wood and a piece of iron and prize the bombs out of the ground. We'd unscrew them and get the phosphorus out – it was one hell of a job to get them to light, and the bombs would fizz and sparkle. We'd make a little trail and get this to fizz. There was a little cap inside the bombs and we'd let all the phosphorus out, then line them up on the fence by the railway line and, with airguns, shoot the explosive caps out of the centre of the bombs. There would be a terrific bang and we thoroughly enjoyed ourselves. I suppose there would have been three or four of us and our parents would have had a fit if they'd known about it.

Mrs Deery was a lady who came down from London, as during the Blitz things got pretty bad. She used to work for Mr Knight, who farmed Cranham Place Farm. She brought her husband and children down here during the Blitz and they lived in the sheds opposite the school. She continued to work for Mr Knight after the war.

John Litton

Territorial Army

Just before the war the Territorial Army came to the farm. They stayed for several weeks and used the meadow, then when the war began we had searchlights there. Some of the men were based in the house – they had the big downstairs room. We were very lucky in that we had very little bomb damage apart from broken windows, probably caused by a blast.

I remember a landmine coming down near North Ockendon Hall, which had to be demolished because so much damage was done. It fell to one side of a straw stack and it blew the straw all over the front of the Hall.

A landmine also fell on our property at the edge of Freemans Wood, which is an ancient wood, and it was probably the blast that cut the trees down to about four feet.

Joy Scott

Candles in the Shelter

I was born in the year the Second World War began, but I can remember hurrying down to our Anderson shelter. We were bombed during the war but all I can remember is seeing a couple of craters, and there were soldiers around. I went to North Ockendon Church School when I was small and, when I went to Gaynes later, I'd wait for the school bus at White Post Corner.

We had a brick-built shelter outside the school which we'd hurry to when we heard the siren. It was purpose-built with no windows so as to avoid falling glass, so we'd go in with candles, and then eat the dripping wax pretending it was chewing gum.

Pam Bonnett

Pam Bonnett and Gwen Bishop (*née* Coates), 1940s.

Home Guard

I was in the Home Guard by the time I was sixteen, as were most of the men in the village who weren't away fighting, and we were often on duty all night. Our headquarters was in the Old White Horse – the owner of the pub had been a captain in the army, so he was put in charge. Our unit, which consisted mostly of farmers and farm workers, met in the cellar and we had a shooting range at the back of the pub where we practised with .22 rifles. Several people from Upminster were in the South Ockendon Home Guard.

There was quite a lot of bombing in North Ockendon, with a landmine destroying North Ockendon Hall. The post office was never hit though. I looked out of the window one morning and saw a German plane machine-gunning some poor chap who was ploughing in a field. That same morning they machine-gunned all the District Line trains going up to London.

They had an AA battery of about 500 men just at the back of the post office and there was a searchlight battery in Fen Lane, where there were about 200 men. They were all in the Territorial Army and had guns but no shells. I used to go in with the papers and have breakfast there.

The men were all in the acting profession and I was in there one day when somebody upset the cook, who retaliated by throwing two knives, and nearly killed him. It transpired that the cook was a knife-thrower in Civvy Street.

Near the army camp at the bottom and just on the other side of Fen Lane, they built a replica of Hornchurch Aerodrome. It was used as a decoy for German fighter planes who were following our boys back to Hornchurch Aerodrome. When our night-fighters came in they used to switch the replica lights on to guide our boys home and when they landed at Hornchurch, they switched them off. They'd then be switched on again and the Germans who'd been trailing our boys would drop their bombs on the replica airfield. Quite a few bombs were dropped there, although we weren't affected too much; but unfortunately Bulphan was bombed considerably.

We had a phone box outside the post office during the war in case we came across spies. There was a switch inside the post office and we were at liberty to listen in to phone calls if we became suspicious.

A plane crashed at the top of Clay Tye Hill and the Home Guard hurried over there. They managed to get the pilot out but couldn't understand what he was trying to tell them. Fortunately somebody came along who spoke German and he yelled, 'He's set the time bomb, so we'd better get out quick.' They all ran off and the plane blew up.

Members of the Auxiliary Fire Service with the manager of Hall Farm, 1940s.

We used to sell all the sweets when they were rationed, and all the groceries. I remember smacking up the butter etc. and people would come in for, say, two ounces of butter or two ounces of sugar, perhaps three rashers of bacon – it was time consuming and a real nuisance. Newspapers kept printing all through the war.

At that time we had to look after ourselves, food-wise. A woman in Fen Lane kept bantams and goats so we were able to have goats' milk, and people would breed pigs and hide them from the food inspectors. People raised rabbits as well – they'd breed tame rabbits for eating. Miss Landers, who lived in the house where the nursing home now stands, had about 300 rabbits.

We were fairly close to Warley Barracks, which was where the permanent army were based, so we saw lots of convoys of lorries and Bren Gun Carriers heading to the docks. The army were the only people who could get petrol in those days, although the farmers had a little.

By the beginning of the war, tractors were beginning to take over from horses and the village changed, because all the men were horsemen.

Peter Coe

Herd of Cattle

I remember one night when we were huddled in the shelter during an air raid and heard this terrible rumbling above us. When the raid was over we discovered the noise was made by a herd of cattle which had escaped from a field.

Gwen Bishop

Four

VILLAGE LIFE

Ivy Dene

Bill and Nancy Coates, who were my mother and father, originally came from
Brixton. They wanted to get away from London so came east and moved into
a cottage in Clay Tye Road, called Ivy Dene. As the family grew they took the
opportunity to move a couple of doors along into the larger Clay Tye Cottage,
which had four bedrooms. Downstairs it had a scullery, living room and a front
room. I had five brothers and one sister and I was born there – in fact I lived there
until I married at the age of eighteen. It was quite primitive with no bathroom
and an outside toilet but we always had gas, so used that for cooking and lighting
etc. I think our water came from a well and there always seemed to be plenty of it.

Above Sign for Clay Tye Cottage.

Right Annie and Bill Coates in Clay Tye Cottage
garden, around 1954.

I remember the gas mantles but I can't remember having oil lamps. There was an old range in the living room which Mum used to blacklead. We had no hot water at all so this was heated on Friday night for our baths. These were taken in a galvanised bath in the kitchen, and as the youngest I went in first. Naturally there were mice around and I can remember putting my coat on and a mouse running out of it.

Pam Bonnett

Post Office

I was born in East Ham, but in 1931 Dad bought the post office in North Ockendon and took the family to live above the shop. The post office was originally an inn so it was quite spacious, having five bedrooms with rooms over three storeys. It was listed because it was very old, so had the appropriate walls made of lath and plaster. We had gas lamps for quite a few years, but electricity was laid on just before the war. There were cesspools in those days ,of course, and no central heating, so days seemed much colder back then. I remember when my father's false teeth froze in a glass overnight.

There were five concrete steps outside the building, a reminder of the days when the post office was an inn, and these were put there so drunken men could mount their horses. North Ockendon was known as the city of the wells, as there are many of them around and most of the water supply in the area came from

Post office, North Ockendon, around 1960.

this source. There are about five wells opposite the Old White Horse pub and between what was then the post office.

The post office also acted as a general store and Dad served behind the counter. He was up at six o'clock each day to see to the newspapers and we'd have all the post deliveries from Bulphan and South Ockendon to deal with. We'd cycle to pick the newspapers up from South Ockendon station, plus the post that came in from Bulphan and South Ockendon, then we'd sort it in the shop and deliver it by bike around North Ockendon. So effectively, it was picked up and taken back – this was in about 1939. We all went everywhere by bike in those days.

Peter Coe

Jowett Car

There was a bus strike in the 1950s which meant I had to walk into Upminster, which took quite a while, so, I decided to go to Gibsons, a scrapyard which sold cheap cars in Billericay. They had an old Jowett and I bought it. It was a 1928 model with a fabric body and two cylinders which were cracked; but I managed to get hold of some welding equipment and made it almost roadworthy and used it all through the bus strike. It was a very rare car and I sold it on to a chap in Leicestershire. About three or four years ago I heard it's in Yarmouth, on display in Caister Castle Motor Museum.

John Litton

John Litton's Jowett car.

Collis Family

Several of my ancestors lived in South Ockendon. In 1819 George Collis married Eliza Ann Norrington at South Ockendon, where he worked as a farm labourer. They had seven children.

Thomas Collis, who was born in 1800, came to South Ockendon about 1831 and opened his ironmonger's shop in West Street. He had seven children and the shop remained open in the village until the mid-twentieth century.

Joseph George Collis, a carpenter, had moved to South Ockendon by 1851 and lodged with one Zacharia Cutts. In 1852 he married Emma Mays, the eighteen-year-old daughter of Samuel Mays, also a carpenter. They lived in West Street, where they had nineteen children. George (he dropped the Joseph) worked as a carpenter and builder and is believed to have been the bandmaster of Aveley Silver Band. When he became too old for building work, he joined Emma in running a sweetshop next to the ironmongers. He died in 1905, aged eighty-three and Emma outlived him by at least five years.

Coral Jeffrey, née Collis

Doughnuts

We had a variety of shops before South Ockendon village grew. Cowley's was the store at the end of the row where you'd put your order in and then collect it later. Mrs Newbury had a little wool shop and also sold clothes. There was a shoe shop in West Road and a little cobbler's in South Road. Mrs Hall had the paper shop. Mr Dawson had the butchers with the slaughterhouse, and there was a lovely baker's. Since we had to be in work early, we'd go in through the back doors and they'd be making the doughnuts.

Yvonne Rampling

Tips

There was a post office in South Ockendon which was run from the station, and the stationmaster was the boyfriend of the postmistress. In those days the postmen kept a book at Christmas in which they recorded their tips.

Peter Coe

West Street, South Ockendon, early 1900s. (Courtesy of Thurrock Museum Collection)

High Street, South Ockendon, looking north. (Courtesy of Thurrock Museum Collection)

Allotments

Dad drove the ambulance for the South Ockendon Hospital for four years. He used to take the patients to Dovercourt for a holiday.

As a schoolboy I used to be at the station at five o'clock in the morning to pick up the papers and take them into the paper shop for sorting. I'd cycle all through the back lanes and up to North Ockendon on my paper round and then I'd collect the money on Saturday mornings.

Dad had an allotment and I've had one in Mollands Lane for fifty years. I used to look after the allotments but there was a falling-out and I gave up. I still grow my veg up there, though, and I've always helped out. Over the years I've dug every allotment on that site. Allotments used to be run by the council but now they're self-run so we look after them ourselves.

Vic Rampling

Benyons

The Benyons built the eight cottages on the Ockendon Road on the stretch that runs down to the Old White Horse public house. The first two semi-detached houses, i.e. Blackbird Cottage, Nos 2, 3 and 4 were made from shuttered concrete, with the sand and ballast for this purpose being dug from the field adjacent to the cottages.

When I was young there was quite a deep dip at the gateway to the field where the ballast had been extracted by hand digging. The area was eventually filled in with spoil obtained from the dredging and enlargement of the moat at Hall Farm. The story goes that Lady Benyon visited the newly built concrete houses and was appalled by them, so the remaining four cottages had to be brick-built. This happened around 1901. I lived at No. 6, The Rowans for over forty years. The tiles on the roofs of many of the buildings in North Ockendon came from the Benyon Estate in Somerset and each one was marked with a small roundel as being made in Somerset. They were quite large tiles, about a foot by eighteen inches, each with around six pointed ridges running lengthwise down the tile. They're quite easy to spot and were on many roofs in the area.

Geoff Jones

St Mary Magdalene School pupils, around 1967/68.

Children's confirmation, St Mary Magdalene church 1968/70 with the Revd Stoffel, the Right Revd Tiarks (Bishop of Chelmsford) and the Revd Steel.

South Ockendon village centre, early 1900s. (Courtesy of Brian Evans)

Peculiars

As a child, I only went to church when I was told, and that would have been to the chapel in Grays. My family was always very religious – it came down through my grandfather – they were members of the Peculiar People. All my aunts and uncles were Peculiar People and my father was one of their lay preachers. When the Peculiar Movement was started in Rochford in the 1800s by James Banyard, it was the first chapel of the new order and a kind of evangelism. The strict Peculiars wore black all the time and were very straight-laced. Some wouldn't allow doctors for their children, but my people weren't like that. The PPs were along the line of the Wesleyans. They were all over Essex and used to collect once a year in a big hall in Chelmsford for a meeting. Some of the chapels are still going but I have an idea they changed their name to Evangelicals. It started to die out after the war but they'd been all over the place.

Eric Jiggens

Accumulator Man

I was friendly with the daughters of the Jameson family, who had Puddledock Farm at the end of Clay Tye Road. They kept cows on the farm and when

I was about ten, the father, who was a very kind man, taught me how to milk one of them.

It was rumoured that one of the families who used to live in the village had come down in status. They had a daughter, Florrie Kraty, who was a bit of an invalid, and she was governess to Nadia Romanowski, who was the daughter of a Russian princess. I can't remember seeing the princess but she lived with the family.

The accumulator man lived in Castle Cottages which are near where the blacksmith lived in North Ockendon. He'd bring a charged accumulator for the radio and take away the used one. His name was Livermore – we just knew him as Sonny Livermore.

Ardale was an approved school in Stifford when I was young, and I remember the boys coming to our fêtes and concerts.

Gwen Bishop

Cliff Place

I was born and grew up at No. 15, Cliff Place, which is just behind the church, so spent a lot of my life in South Ockendon. My father was born on Bulphan Fen, where I now live, and my mother was born in South Ockendon. When they were first married, my parents lived in one of the old cottages in West Street, but the London County Council pulled down all the houses around there when the new estate was built. I was born in January 1933 and there were six children in our family. Back then, there wasn't much for us to do except get into mischief.

Ockendon started to change just after the war – it's not as I remember it – there's no village life now.

Eric Jiggens

Three-wheeler Car

I had a Morgan three-wheeler when I was about nineteen and nearly killed myself in it. Waterworks Corner in Warley was a much tighter bend in those days and I was racing with another fellow when we crashed at sixty miles an hour. I was told I skidded up the bank and the car turned over. We walked away with cuts and bruises and more sense, and to this day I never exceed the speed limit. This happened in the late '40s.

But I was able to mend the car and eventually sold it to an American, Dr Milton R. Roth, who came from California. I drove it to King George V Dock in London

South Ockendon shops, early 1900s.

High Street, South Ockendon, looking south, early 1900s. (Courtesy of Thurrock Museum Collection)

myself and when I got as far as the traffic lights in Rainham it was pouring with rain and the engine, which was at the front of the car, stalled. A lady in the hairdressers on the other side of the road saw me drying myself and the car out and brought me a cup of tea. I continued my journey and was able to see the car on its way to the States on a Royal Mail vessel.

John Litton

Lascars

I used to go into South Ockendon once a week to buy the groceries from the little shop on the corner called Cowley's. I'd select what I wanted and then the shop would deliver it.

The boats used to pull into Tilbury docks in those days and the Lascars (Indian or south-east Asian sailors) used to come round the houses selling goods from a suitcase – dusters, scarves and things.

My husband's father was a blacksmith, as was his father. My father-in-law was brought up in North Ockendon and the whole generation before him were blacksmiths. The grandfather put them all in blacksmiths' shops around the area – Warley, North and South Ockendon, St Mary's Lane, Corbets Tey, etc.

My husband was John Bernard Cressey and I met him through my brother. We married in 1948 and my son was born in 1952.

Evelyn Cressey

Tramps

Mrs Cast had the bakers, and all the tramps used to call there – in those days there were lots of tramps on the road. They could only stay in the workhouses for one night, so they'd go to Orsett, then to Billericay and from there on to Oldchurch, and back to Orsett, staying one night in each place. The workhouse people would give them tickets to buy bread etc.

Peter Coe

King's Head

There was a pub called the King's Head in South Ockendon where the working men's club is now, and all the farm lads used to collect in there. My uncle was a drinker, but a happy drinker – he could sing all the old songs.

Mr Brown was the vicar at the time and he was so popular that after he left South Ockendon, the locals used to run coaches up to Cambridge to see him. My grandmother had eight children from three marriages and I had two aunties and two uncles who worked in the hospital.

Jim McGillivray

Dr Mac

Our doctor was based in South Ockendon. His name was MacPherson, but known to us as Dr Mac. He smoked like a chimney and we could hear him coughing while we were in the surgery waiting room. He was tall and thin and he was a character, and very popular. He also took teeth out and gave injections etc., this would be in 1939.

In those days, the only people who had a car were the vicar and the doctor.

Mr Cole, the farmer at Puddledock Farm, was a special constable during the war and I used to deliver his papers. He'd often come into the shop to chat with my Dad. I remember he repaired the big clock we had on the wall. We were quite a little community those days.

Towards the end of our time in the post office we used to get our cakes from Garons at Southend. The building was eventually left to deteriorate as it was listed and there's a new house on the site now.

Anglers at Puddledock Farm.

The postman who dealt with the mailbox by Fisher's Farm near the railway bridge used to say he collected it every day, but we decided to check after three months. We opened the box up and all the letters fell out where he'd not collected them.

One of the Fisher family – who farmed at Manor Farm – was married to Joe Pigg, who had the big business in Grays but lived in Orsett. He used to come out to North and South Ockendon delivering bread, meat, vegetables, everything. But one day he had a row with his staff, so sacked them all and closed the business down.

Peter Coe

Matriarch

Mum was the matriarch of Clay Tye and was always in attendance when babies were born.

I can remember climbing trees and falling out and going gleaning for corn, which they grew in the next field. We'd be allowed to collect the grain for Dad's chickens as our cottage belonged to the farmer, Mr Marks, who owned Clay Tye farm.

There was a shirt factory in St Mary's Lane and Dad worked there at one time, but his last job was to help lay the drainage at the special school in Harwood Hall Lane in Upminster. Most buses ran hourly and Mum used to take me into Grays, where we'd go to the beach in summer. We'd also go into Upminster and catch the train to Southend.

The post office was on the left-hand side of North Road, just before you get to Fen Lane, and was owned by Peter Coe's father. We used to buy our sweets there too but the building has since been pulled down and there's a new house there now.

Further on, just past Fen Lane, was the bakery where we'd get our bread. The baker's was owned by Mr Cast and the old house, called The Bakery, is still there.

Milk was delivered by Kate, the milkmaid. We had groceries delivered by Cowley's and they came from the shop in South Ockendon. Matthews came with the flour – they were millers from Maldon.

I was christened, confirmed and married in St Mary Magdalene church. We knew everybody in North Ockendon and most of our activities took place on the rectory lawn at that time; but the village atmosphere has disappeared now.

Pam Bonnett

Children at the St Mary Magdalene nativity play, 1960s.

Cuckoo Lane

Although I was born in Lewisham, I had an extended family in South Ockendon so often visited the area as a child.

My aunt spent her later years in the house next door to my wife and me in South Road, but originally she lived in one of the Gunarys' farmhouses in North Ockendon. Her husband worked on the farm and they had a tied cottage in North Road, near to the Old White Horse. They didn't have running water in the house – just a tap outside – and the toilet was in the garden. Gas wasn't laid on, so she cooked on an old-fashioned stove. When the farm was sold they had to leave the cottage in North Ockendon, so came to live in South Ockendon.

I had a cousin who'd never ventured out of North Ockendon, but when he was called up during the Second World War he was sent to Burma where, being a farm boy, he looked after the mules. He was never the same when he came home. When our house became available it was in a bit of a state as the old lady who owned it only lived in one room, but my brother recommended my wife and I buy it, as it was structurally sound. My brother, who was in the building trade for years, made the house habitable and modernised it, so we moved in — that was forty-seven years ago. We bought the house outright for £2,450 in 1966.

South Ockendon signal box, around 1920. (Courtesy of Brian Evans)

Before the new estate was built, there were orchards at the back of Quince Tree House with Cuckoo Lane running through them to South Ockendon railway station. My Uncle Harry had permission to keep his chickens in the orchards – there were hundreds of them running about. Everybody kept chickens and once a week the man would come down from Harold Wood to deliver chicken feed to the people.

It was said that South Ockendon railway station was the prettiest in England as it won a competition for the sign – South Ockendon in flowers. It was always lovely in summer as the stationmaster turned the embankment into a garden – I remember the bluebells.

I used to go pea picking for a week at a time – usually when I was off school and got sixpence or sometimes a shilling a sack, depending on the size.

Jim McGillivray

Five

AT LEISURE

Robert Middlemas, OBE

As a boy I belonged to the Scouts and in 1938, in view of the Munich Crisis, it was thought unwise to set up our summer camp too far from home. Because of this, permission was sought and granted to pitch our tents on a 100-acre field alongside Clay Tye Farm in North Ockendon. Later this was to become known as the Fair Play field. The field was owned by William Martin and we camped right at the top of the hill but had to go down to the large barn for water. We'd buy sweets from Coe's (the post office) and a little shop in Clay Tye Road.

Sometimes buses bringing children from the East End would be on the field, and they'd invite us to join in with their games. We particularly liked to watch the Punch & Judy show.

We were already aware of these children as we'd be in the Scouts' hut, which was on the hill leading to St Andrew's church on the Hornchurch Road, and could hear them singing and the old buses changing gear, as they struggled to get up the hill. We'd rush out to watch them go by.

The children were there by courtesy of Mr Robert Middlemas, OBE, who lived locally in Cranham Court in St Mary's Lane – it's now a nursing home. He was given the OBE for services in the First World War but I don't know the detail.

He was involved in a cigar importing company of some note with premises in Mansell Street, in the City of London. The business encompassed the sale of the finest tobacco, cigars and cigarettes and traded under the name of B. Morris & Sons Ltd.

Mr Middlemas was also a racehorse owner and philanthropist and, by being familiar with that location, he would have had ample opportunity to see the poverty in the East End, so came up with the idea of taking some of the children out of their environment to spend a day in the open air. He was a friend of Lord Ashfield, who was the founder of the London Passenger Transport Board, so it was probably through this connection that he was able to buy his first old bus. He took the children from several East End homes and charitable organisations, for a day out in the countryside at North Ockendon. As the popularity of the scheme increased he had to provide more buses; in 1937 he had seven and by 1938 his fleet had increased to ten. In that year, 50,000 children were catered for, with each bus carrying sixty-five children to and fro. The buses were very old so he found it necessary to hold two in reserve. He had friends in high places who gave generously to his schemes.

MORRIS'S XMAS FANCIES FOR 1939.			15

MAandPA

| Combination contains 1 Corona size Cigar, 4 Half Corona size Cigars. 10 mixed tipped Virginia Cigarettes | ... | per doz. | 28/- |
| Minimum Retail Price | ... | per box | 3/3 |

EL GRANDILLA DE LUXE CIGARS

5 Cigars packed in leatherette box per doz. boxes			28/6
Retail Price	...	per box	3/3
In Outers containing 1 doz. Cigars		per doz.	5/6
Retail Price	...	each	7d.
In Upright Cabinet. 25's	...	per 100	45/6

Each Cigar packed on end in separate Pliapbane Container
Special Quotations for Quantities

LAS CRUZANAS CORONAS CIGARS

A full size Corona Cigar which sells at 7¼d. each

List Prices. In Wood Boxes. 50's	per 100	45/6
25's	,,	47/-
10's	per doz.	59/6
5's	,,	30/-
In Card Slides. 5's	,,	27/6
2's	,,	12/3

10 Cigars packed in cedarwood pocket folding box. A Specially Fine Value Cigar for Christmas Trade.

| Retail minimum price | ... | per case | 6/6 |

All Cigar Prices are subject to 2½% discount

Special Reduction for Quantities

1939 Christmas catalogue of cigars sold by Mr Middlemas' company.

By sheer coincidence, years later, I went to work for the firm who did Morris & Son's printing work. Although Mr Middlemas was dead by this time, the company was still operating, so I got to know of his generosity and kindness through my colleagues, and to learn how well respected he was.

His horses were stabled at Newmarket and he won the Victory Cup and the Queen Elizabeth Cup with a horse named Fair Play, so I can only think the field was named in the horse's honour.

I understand that after the war he revived the idea of giving the children a day out by hiring boats on the river. Mr Middlemas died in 1951 at the age of eighty-four.

Russell Spencer

Selling Sweets

Another person I remember from the war is Mr Middlemas, who lived at Cranham Court. He used to bring children down from London so they could have a day in the country. He began by using one bus but eventually there was a fleet of them – I think he financed everything himself. The buses would turn into the chase which was alongside our house, and then drive into Fairplay farm. Mum set herself up a little sweet shop in the front room and she'd sell sweets to the children.

I went to a party at Mr Middlemas' home and was in awe at how large it was. The room we used had a large glass dome, which seemed amazing to a small girl.

Pam Bonnett

Punch & Judy

In the 1930s, Mr Middlemas from Cranham Court instigated a scheme whereby he could bring deprived children from inner London out to North Ockendon for a day in the country. He, with the help of some generous friends, began with one busload and when the idea proved successful, other buses were added, which meant they were able to bring thousands of children down to play in the open air in the summer. Several East End organisations were associated with the scheme. The fleet of buses was operated by three retired London Transport drivers. Each bus could hold seventy-five children, who were watched over by two attendants. The day was spent at Fairplay Farm and during term time they were collected after school and taken home at about half-past eight, although during the month of August they spent the whole day here. This all took place in a field of some

Fair Play bus, around the 1930s.

100 acres which belonged to Mr Martin at the time – my grandfather didn't buy the farm until the 1950s.

There was a large barn on the field and during August the children ate their packed lunch in there; a little shop was set up where they could buy sweets. They ran around the field playing games and often entertainment was laid on, a favourite being a Punch & Judy show. At three o'clock they were given ice-creams, buns and lemonade.

The buses were kept in one of the barns and until quite recently I used to find pennies the children dropped in the field. As a youngster, I found lots of balls in the hedges. In one of my sheds there's a brick structure, which is where the little sweet shop was built for them. Mind you, they weren't all sweetness and light. One of my aunts told me the children would hang out of the windows and spit at the village children.

Steve White

Pitt's Van

I remember when Mr Middlemas brought the children down from London by bus to Fairplay farm, so they could have a day in the fresh air. Since she had seven children, Mum needed to be inventive where money was concerned and was aware these children had been given pennies to spend. So she found herself a large laundry basket and filled it with sweets to sell to the children. I remember Pitt's van from Brentwood brought her the sweets, but a lady who had a sweet shop in St Mary's Lane used to advise Mum on what to get. Later Mum made hot dinners for the bus drivers – she'd been in service so was an extremely good cook.

Gwen Bishop

Handbells

I began playing handbells when I was about eleven. We practised in the Reading Room and the bells were stored there in a specially made compartment. A lot of the bells were bought by the villagers and we played by numbers, so if the leader called out the wrong number we were stuck! Don Rogers is the only villager I can remember who owned his own bell which he later donated to the village. We used to play at the church and the socials that were held in the hall at that time. Stan Gunn lived at the back of the school – he was our captain and looked after the music.

Handbell players, led by Don Reed.

The group ceased playing for some years but reformed in the 1990s. Brian Beech, who was a church member, became captain and arranged the music. When he left, another church member, Don Reed, took over and we starting branching out into old people's homes and church halls. We went to a home in Grays that cared for youngsters who were either bedridden or in wheelchairs, and we also played at Tilbury Fort for a special occasion. We were even interviewed by BBC Radio Essex, as a result of which we were invited to their studio to play for one of their programmes.

We applied for a lottery grant to spend money on the bells some years ago, as the leather handles were floppy and other small repairs were needed. We received quite a nice sum so were able to buy some more bells.

I played with the present team for thirteen years and left twelve years ago when other commitments took over. I thoroughly enjoyed my time with them and missed the sessions. The handbell ringing team continues to perform to this day and is now stronger than ever.

Pam Bonnett

More Handbells

The North Ockendon handbell ringers use the Reading Room provided by Richard Benyon for practise on Tuesday evenings. The handbell ringers were formed during the Second World War by the church tower ringers, because church bells were only to be rung if an invasion occurred, so Don Rogers and his fellow ringers bought a set of handbells so they could still practise 'method' ringing.

After the war they were resurrected and Stan Gunn, a well-known Essex handbell ringer who had recently moved to North Ockendon, and decided to set up a group. The group carried on later under Don Reed and has, over the years, greatly increased the number of bells. It's gone from strength to strength and now raises money for charities and plays for clubs, etc.

Geoff Jones

Lantern Slides

When we lived in Ivy Dene, my father used to put a sheet on the wall above the stairs and give us little lantern slideshows. My mother was very sociable and she used to arrange concerts on the stage in the school.

Pam Bonnett

Entertainment

My parents having parted company, I arrived in South Ockendon aged five years with my mother, whose maternal family had lived in the village since at least the 1700s. Indeed, there are two graves in the churchyard of the family from that time. Therefore she came back to South Ockendon, where her mother, brother and one of her sisters were living.

Entertainment in the village varied to a degree. The South Ockendon Choral Society practised in the schoolroom of the Wesleyan Chapel and held their concerts in the Congregational church hall. Sometimes a dance was held in that same hall. Whichever body of people staged a show, it was usually there or in the Oddfellows Hall. The Boys Brigade practised in the church hall and at times paraded through the village. There was also a South Ockendon Silver Band, which I only heard once, at a fête in the recreation ground at the back of the cemetery. A fair would sometimes come to Collar Makers Row, opposite what was the rectory. There were three sweet shops, a baker's, grocers, greengrocers, two butchers, post office, saddler, blacksmith, cycle shop, garage, ironmongers, oilman etc., and a little private school in West Road run by Mrs and Miss Shipman. And there were four public houses.

I can remember a windmill at the end of Hall Lane where there was also a moat, in the middle of which had stood the very ancient manor house of the Saltonstall family. A large monument to this family is in the church. Should one continue along Hall Lane, past the moat, one would eventually come out on Bulphan (Bulvan) Fen, quite a long way. Today South Ockendon bears no resemblance to what it used to be.

On Saturday afternoons my mother used to like to go to the pictures in Grays – ten pence for her and five pence for me.

With regard to entertainment there was also Kay Geden's tap-dancing troupe, who used to put on a concert in the church hall at times. They were all children who tap-danced and did acrobatics. Kay's mother always accompanied them on the piano. I thought they were great and their signature tune was 'Happy Feet'.

Ann Staff

Parties

I used to go to parties in a large house in Clay Tye Road and got to know a girl called Millicent Martin quite well. Later she became quite famous in the entertainment industry but I believe she went to live in America.

Pam Bonnett

Dance Hall

The Martins had the dance hall in Romford and they lived in the house where the nursing home now stands. Millicent Martin came to live with them when her parents split up.

Peter Coe

Sports and Social Club

Dad started the Sports and Social Club together with Stan Coates, who was very energetic, and they got together good cricket and football teams. It's still an appropriate meeting point for the village.

Land Army Girls and pupils of North Ockendon School, 1942.

We all met in the Old White Horse on Friday and Saturday nights, where we mostly played darts. Along with the locals, there were a couple of Land Army Girls helping on the farms, and we made our own fun.

Peter Coe

Rectory Meadow

The village functions were held on the rectory meadow in Church Lane and there was a hall called the Reading Room where we had socials etc. All sorts of activities went on there.

We had a fête on the lawn every year and Mum and Mrs Cranfield (even though they were great friends, Mum called her Mrs Cranfield for years) used to run the linen stall where they'd sell pillowcases, tablecloths etc. that they'd made. They did the teas in the rectory kitchen – I can remember them pumping the water up to the kitchen.

We had a tea party in the Reading Room for the Coronation and always played on the rectory meadow when we were at school. We played stool-board at school.

I was in the choir at church and one of my brothers started the Sports and Social Club. It was when they started playing football and cricket that he brought

North Ockendon village children at the summer picnic, 1960s.

along a school friend who was to become my husband. I watched cricket and helped with the teas, and every year we had a match with girls against the boys.

Pam Bonnett

Dances at The Colony

We used to go to dances at the South Ockendon Hospital. We called it The Colony at that time. They had a very good dance hall and served lovely refreshments at half-time – all the locals used to go. They had some good bands there and often Harry Gold and his Pieces of Eight would supply the music.

Peter Coe

Cinema

I worked in London when I was fifteen so, since there was nothing in Ockendon except for pubs, we went up to London for entertainment. We went to Grays to the cinema, of course – where there were the Ritz and the State. We teenagers would pay half-fare on the bus and then get into category eighteen at the pictures.

Margaret Abboyi

Six

FARMS AND
FARM WORKERS

North Ockendon Farms

The farms that existed when I was a lad, and up to the 1970s, are now mainly owned by one farmer, but years ago the individual farms were nearly all producing market garden crops, which were raised for the London wholesale markets of Stratford, Borough and Covent Garden. In my younger days, each year at harvest time, the North Ockendon Sports and Social Club held a harvest supper in the Reading Room for all the local farm workers. At that time we limited the number to about sixty people, as we couldn't seat more. The incumbent of the church was always invited, but invariably left after the food and guest speaker, with the excuse of expecting a telephone call, as he was aware that some of the jokes and entertainment got a bit raunchy. I went around to all the farmers to get donations for the cost of the food etc., as the workers didn't pay and in that way I got to know all the farms and owners.

Cyril Gunary owned Hall Farm, and before North Ockendon Hall was bombed, a Mr and Mrs Murley and a Mr and Mrs Catton lived there. The two ladies were sisters of Cyril Gunary, with George Murley working in the City of London. Cyril Gunary farmed White Post Farm and he lived in the farmhouse with his wife and two daughters.

Redcrofts Farm on the Ockendon Road was farmed by Ernest Dennis.

Mr Attenborough farmed at Grove Farm on the Ockendon Road and the house and buildings are now company offices. The farm had quite large orchards with plum and apple trees, which ran along the Ockendon Road from Redcrofts to Grove. As well as market gardening they had fine rhubarb fields and I used to work there during the school holidays, picking fruit. I also used this as a stopgap between leaving school and serving an apprenticeship with F.A. Secretts, who were market gardeners based at Walton-on-Thames in Surrey.

The orchards were grubbed out following the war and a lot of the farm was dug for sand and ballast by Olley & Son.

Part of the original Corner Farm on Fen Lane is now known as the Top Meadow Golf Course. Years ago this was always known as Mill Meadow, for the simple reason that a windmill once stood at the top of the hill. During the war, another sandpit was dug at the top of Mill Meadow, at one end of which there was quite a high cliff area. This was used as a rifle range by the local Home Guard.

Home Farm in Fen Lane was farmed by Jack Haydock, followed by his son, Robert. Jack was also well known for his dealing in agricultural machinery, which he bought and sold. He was a familiar figure at farm sales, particularly at the Cambridge auction market.

Forge Field on Main Road was an acre of land owned by Harry Cressey, the blacksmith, at the rear of the forge. My Dad, Walter Jones, and I rented it when I came back from National Service in 1955. It was registered as a smallholding and used for intensive salad and vegetable growing. Mains water was laid on for irrigation purposes, and a 100-foot-span Dutch light, structured mobile greenhouse was erected, together with a large 100-foot-wide greenhouse which was unfortunately destroyed in a violent gale before it was completed. Material from it was used to make a smaller low-span greenhouse near the same site. The field was still rented and used by my father as an allotment after his retirement in 1970 until his death in 1994.

Glebe Farm on Church Lane was owned by the church. It was usually rented by farmers and incorporated into their own farms. It included the meadow opposite the school, which was used by the Sports and Social Club for cricket and football, with the Reading Room being used as a club house and changing room.

George Knight rented The Glebe for years as part of Cranham Place Farm; it was then taken over by Cyril Gunary as part of Hall Farm. When Hall Farm was sold, my father took over the rent and it was used for market gardening until his retirement. I worked with Dad from the beginning but it became very difficult to make a living, and the whole area went into decline. The farms were taken over for more arable crops such as potatoes, corn and sugar beet, which had a dramatic effect on the whole village of North Ockendon. Most of the houses in the village were tied to the farms and used only for workers. The six cottages on Church Lane were tied to Hall Farm, and the eight cottages on the Ockendon Road belonged to White Post and Hall Farms. Some dwellings near to the railway were tied to Cranham Place Farm. All the cottages were later sold to private owners. Number 6, Ockendon Road, which I had rented since 1958, was sold to Romford Stadium, who'd had the greyhound kennels built on Ockendon Road. The land was originally part of White Post Farm.

Fortunately I was able to buy my house from them as a sitting tenant, and I lived there until I moved to Beccles in 2006.

Geoff Jones

Dynasty

My great-grandfather, Sam Gunary, was born in 1847 and died in 1930. He had five sons – George, Charles, Harry, Ernie and Stan – and it was Sam who created the Gunary farming dynasty.

It's possibly a family legend that he began farming when he bought a growing field of turnips at the corner of Bennetts Castle Lane in Dagenham. He worked non-stop for three weeks so he could take the turnips up to Covent Garden to sell them. The only sleep he had was on the return journey, as the horses always knew their way home. Apparently, he made so much money, he bought seven acres from his landlord and that was the beginning of the Gunary 'empire'.

Charles Gunary, the second son who was my grandfather, began farming at Dagenham but when the Ford Motor Company bought the land from the council, the farmers had to move elsewhere. He bought a farm at Stapleford Abbots and subsequently bought some more land at Tendring. My father, being the eldest son, became the salesman at Covent Garden and I followed in his footsteps. We built the business up and I was there for fifty-one years selling fruit and produce. Rather than just selling produce from the farm, we ended up taking fruit from all over the world, as we'd acquired large warehouses for storage.

After the war there were three businesses operating with nine partners – S. Gunary & Sons, G. Gunary & Sons and Charles Gunary and, between them, they farmed about 3,000 acres in Essex and the borders of Suffolk.

George was the eldest and his business was run by Cyril, Don and Lewis. Then there was S. Gunary & Sons, which was carried on by Harry, Ernie and Stanley. My grandfather's business was carried on by my father, also named Bill, and by Harold and Dennis Gunary. So there were three families who descended from Sam Gunary. They're all deceased now, of course.

George, Sam's eldest, decided to branch out on his own and bought Primrose Farm in Barley Lane, Goodmayes. It was on the opposite side of the road to the mental hospital – the theory was that hospitals should be surrounded by plenty of land, to ensure a good supply of fresh vegetables.

George was a very go-ahead sort of man and when Ilford was made a borough in the late 1920s, he became the second Mayor of Ilford. When King George

Hospital opened in Newbury Park in the 1930s, both George and Charles Gunary became governors.

He subsequently sold Primose Farm for £13,000 when he bought North Ockendon Hall in the mid-1930s. From the proceeds, he gave £2,000 to each of his five children, bought his wife a fur coat and then treated himself to a Daimler. The Daimler was adapted for use as an ambulance during the Second World War. He and Annie, his wife, moved into North Ockendon Hall and later he bought White Post Farm, where Cyril and Sybil lived.

Harry Gunary, who farmed in Rainham, was a prominent pig farmer but I'm not sure if they had any pigs at North Ockendon. They had pigs at Fordham, and over at Stapleford we had pigs and a dairy herd as well. When growing vegetables a good nutritious soil is needed, so plenty of dung was used rather than just chemical fertilisers. Also, when the manure was ploughed into the ground, the content of straw assisted soil drainage. Even in those days, they learned from experience. George was very clever – he had an excellent eye and was a good judge. He'd buy growing crops from farmers, particularly peas, and take his own gang of seasonal workers to pick them. He'd sell them in the London market and in that way earned money by dealing, as well as from his own produce. I think it was his judgement and energy that made his the most successful of the three businesses.

North Ockendon Hall was bombed during the war and, when George died, his three sons encouraged their mother, Annie, to buy a bungalow in Ardleigh Green Road, Hornchurch.

North Ockendon Show, around the 1940s.

George was buried in the North Ockendon church and masses of people attended the funeral service, as he had his finger in so many pies during his lifetime. His body was taken to church in a cart from the farm, drawn by two of his working horses. It was a very elaborate affair, with the horses groomed and the cart all painted and polished specially for the occasion.

Cyril had two daughters, Don had one son who didn't like farming and Lewis had three daughters, so there was no third generation to take the businesses on. For that reason, the farms were eventually sold.

Bill Gunary

Baldwin's Farm

My maternal grandfather became manager of Baldwin's Farm in North Ockendon in the 1920s. My mother was the daughter of the house and met my father when he went to work on the farm. When she and Dad married, they moved into the farmhouse and lived with my grandparents. Dad took over as farm manager when my grandfather retired, although he continued to live with us. I was the first of five children and we were all born on the farm, albeit there were quite large gaps between when each of us was born. As a child, my grandfather lived in Corbets Tey.

The timber-framed farmhouse was built in the sixteenth century and was moated. It had three main rooms at the front, both upstairs and downstairs. At the back there were another three bedrooms upstairs, and downstairs were the kitchens, pantries and a bathroom, with the office being at one end of the house, where my grandfather did the accounts and paid the men.

The roof at the back of the house was made of slate, and the front was tiled.

We had no electricity, nor gas and no water, so we used an outside WC and our water was pumped from a well in the garden, although by the time we left we had flushing toilets. For lighting we used oil lamps and candles, and we had pressure lamps. We always had plenty of hot water as it was heated by a very large range in the kitchen.

The washing was done by hand and a flat iron used for ironing. By the time we left the farm we had a generator, but it wasn't very efficient.

My grandmother was a marvellous cook; although my mother was also an excellent cook who'd won prizes for it at school. We had our own vegetable patch but were at liberty to take what we wanted from the fields. There were rabbits around and we kept chickens so there was always plenty of meat.

Our address was Baldwin's Farm, Upminster; but we were in the North Ockendon parish of Thurrock. The reason we had an Upminster address was influenced by the fact we were part of the Stubbers estate and the owner, Champion Russell, found he could get his post more easily from Upminster than from Thurrock. Later Mr Gay took the farm over.

Mrs Russell used to come down regularly to inspect the house, as was usual for landlords back then. The Russells also held shooting parties which were organised by Stubbers. They'd invite local business men in the area to the shoot because in those days there was plenty of partridge and pheasant around. They used our office for the lunch and Mrs Russell would bring down all the food, china and cutlery etc. and I suppose my grandmother was asked to help.

The milk was delivered by Vaughns, who had the dairy in South Ockendon. In West Road there was an ironmongers owned by a Mr Collis and halfway down the same road was a shop called Gurnett's. There were two brothers in the ironmongers shop and they used to go round the houses selling paraffin from a lorry. They also sold such things as nails and saucepans. If you had a hole in a kettle you'd take it to them and they'd repair it in the yard at the side of the shop.

We used to get most of our meat from Holt's, which was a high-class butchers in North Street, South Ockendon village. Mr Holt had a small abattoir at the back of the shop so he could slaughter his own animals, thus ensuring his meat was fresh. The abattoir didn't operate commercially – it was only for his use.

Our horses were shoed by Coe's in Corbets Tey village because Mr Gay owned Sunnings Farm as well, so it was convenient to get all the horses shoed in the same place.

Baldwin's was an arable farm but we had three pairs of horses and three singles. They were all working horses for the ploughing etc. and were needed to take the produce to the market. They'd leave in the evening and the horses would know exactly where to go. Sometimes on the way home the horsemen would fall asleep so were in danger of the horse turning round and going back to London again, as they knew the route so well. They were also familiar with the other horses going to market and would try to walk alongside them.

Later, bullocks were brought to us by train so we could feed them up. They were delivered to South Ockendon station and the men would drive them to the farm.

I'd have been about twelve when I'd ride my bike to the station with the men, and it was my job to cycle between the bullocks to stop them from entering gateways into the wrong farms.

The men who worked on the farm used to stop for lunch at midday and always ate it in the stable. In the winter they'd be put to clearing ditches and cutting hedges.

We left the farm in 1970 when my father retired. The M25 was coming – the area had been surveyed before the war and stakes were put in the ditches to mark where the new motorway would go; but when the war came about my father had to knock the stakes out – goodness knows why. When the M25 was eventually built, the farm would have been reduced by about 25 per cent but we'd already left by then and it was being dug for gravel anyway.

The family had been on the farm since my mother was four years old, and she also went to school in South Ockendon. In the school holidays she had to walk to Stubbers to get skimmed milk for our family and the lady who lived in the nearby cottage, which we called the tin house. In those days we all drank skimmed milk, as the cream was used to make butter. Mum used to go to the end of the lane and across the park, always apprehensive as she passed the geese they kept at Stubbers because she was scared of them. The geese were there to keep the grass down.

We had a large pond in the garden at Baldwin's. It had ducks on it which were always at the mercy of local foxes and I remember one year the pond froze over. One of the workmen encouraged me to skate on it and my father was not amused.

At certain times of the year several Gypsy caravans would appear near Ham River and we'd pass their little encampment on our way to school. An elderly lady who wore a white apron appeared to be in charge – for some reason she always asked us the time – and the others would be whittling away, making their dolly pegs to sell from house to house.

Joy Scott

Herdsman

My father worked at Drakes Farm, which is off Fen Lane. He was a cowman for a good few years and we lived in a tied cottage in Dunnings Lane, near the farm.

Dad was a herdsman so it was his job to do everything involving the welfare of the cows, including milking. He'd get up very early each morning to start milking at six o'clock and was usually finished by nine, when he'd come back to the house to have his breakfast. The cows would be taken out to pasture then brought back in for milking again at about four in the afternoon. When the milk was in the churn it was taken to the bottom of the road and tankers came round to collect it every morning – this would have been in the '50s. I used to help Dad as a child, because when the cows were in the cowsheds they had to be cleaned out.

All the farms round here had cattle in those days but you see hardly any now. The only farm I know that keeps animals is at Horndon-on-the-Hill, where they have sheep.

Life was hard for my mother, since she'd been brought up in London and the cottage was quite isolated. Naturally, we had no modern appliances: in fact no electricity, nor gas and she cooked on an open fire. There was no lighting so we used paraffin lamps. She'd boil up the washing on Mondays and iron it with an old flat iron on Tuesdays. We had to go into Laindon for our shopping, which was a long drag. I know it was usual for lorries to go round to the farms with supplies, but none came to us in Dunnings Lane. I had to walk to school so I'd make my way through Dunnings Lane then along Fen Lane, then into China Lane to get to Bulphan School – which must have been about three or four miles.

Dad was sixty-three when he died and we think it was partly due to the fact he was gassed during the First World War. He could never drink anything fizzy, although he coped well enough. He served in the Second World War as well, and was in the army for thirty-two years so he was in his late 40s when he started work as a herdsman. We were living in London and I think his health was the reason he wanted to work out in the country.

We went from Drakes Farm to Buckenham Farm at Horndon-on-the Hill. We lived opposite what is now a golf course and when I left school I worked on the railway as an engine cleaner at Stratford, but my parents eventually bought a house in Ilford.

Years later, my wife and I lived in Manor Park but decided to sell up about ten or twelve years ago and came to live in South Ockendon – our house is built on the site of the old Co-op Dairy.

Ted Barton

Shoeing the Geese

By the beginning of the war, tractors were beginning to take over from horses and the village changed because all the men were horsemen. You'd see a team of horses coming off the fields with a sack over their backs to keep them warm at about four o'clock. There would be somebody in the stables to clean and feed them, as it's said that when a man ploughed an acre of land he walked ten miles, so those horses really did work.

There were about three big farms, all producing vegetables for the local market. It nearly all went by lorry with two or three wagons pulling out from the yards, some to Spitalfields and some to Covent Garden. The wagons would be pulled by two horses and the drivers would sometimes fall asleep. They'd be stopped by police and woken up as they went into the East End and they'd also be watched for such things as defective paraffin or gas lamps. There was a hive of activity around agriculture in those days.

There was a farm at the foot of Fen Lane run by the Haydock family, who kept livestock. When they needed to sell the geese and ducks in Romford Market, there was only one way to take them and that was on foot. So, they'd lay down tar followed by a stretch of sand and run the geese through it so they had something solid to walk on. This practise was known as 'shoeing the geese' because they'd have to be driven by road.

Peter Coe

Manor Farm

My father, Arthur P. Mee, bought Manor Farm in May 1969. He'd been the tenant since 1961 and when he and my mother married in 1962, they moved into the farmhouse and I was born a year later. The farmhouse was built in the late 1800s/early 1900s. My mother was from the borders of Stock and Billericay and she came from a lengthy farming background. She was descended from Scottish farmers, with both her grandfather and father having been dairy farmers. Her father came down to Essex from Scotland with his father in the 1930s and they brought their animals with them.

Manor Farmhouse, 1930.

My father was an eighth-generation farmer in South Essex who became tenant farmer to Caleb Rayner in 1961. Manor Farm had formed part of the Benyon estate when it was sold to pay for death duties in 1937. It was bought by F.W. Surridge and sold to Caleb Rayner in 1952 when the tenant, Mr F.M. Fisher, passed away.

The Benyon estate had been massive – in Essex it encompassed land beyond Warley, South Ockendon, Bulphan and Cranham, into Romford and Gidea Park, etc.

I've lived all my life on the farm, apart from periods when I was away at school. Farming is in my blood and all I ever wanted to do, so I spent most of my school holidays working here. I first went to a preschool that was held in Boyd Hall in Cranham, and then to a little school in Butts Green Road until I was seven, when I went to boarding school. I went on to a farming college when I was sixteen.

We're an arable farm and the crops we grow have changed over the years. Whereas when I left school we were growing wheat, barley, oats, peas, potatoes, sugar beet and probably more, we now grow wheat, barley and rapeseed, which we sell through merchants. The crops are a world commodity now and things have changed quite quickly. Our field size of about fourteen acres is quite small and this is due to having more roads, buildings, the railway line etc. in the area – most farmers' fields would be almost double that.

Stuart Mee (left) with his brother Richard, Manor Farm, around 1976.

In my father's day (say, in the 1950s) he'd use pesticides that contained – possibly – nicotine, arsenic or paraffin, but it was all that was available to control pests. Anything used as a pesticide these days would have been tested over a number of years to ascertain it is benign to the environment. If proved not to be so, it would be removed very quickly.

Over the years we've developed a farm shop, where we sell potatoes and eggs as well as animal feed and all things associated with horses and other pets. We still sell our own wheat in there and there's been a marked increase in demand for chicken feed these past years.

My father was involved with a group of about four people who administered the Poyntz charity for years. The Poyntz family were generous benefactors to the area and, amongst its other interests, the charity owns some bungalows which are there for people connected with the village who might be in need.

Stuart Mee

Thrashers

My grandfather moved from Rettendon to North Ockendon in 1919–20. He came here when Winches of South Ockendon closed down their thrashing business, so a round opened in North Ockendon. There wasn't too much work in Rettendon at the time so my grandfather took the opportunity to move his machinery here, although he still worked under the company name of White Brothers of Rettendon Common. Contractors, such as my grandfather, would own their thrashing equipment and traction engine, which they'd use as they worked round the farms.

At first, Granddad rented a house called Blackbird cottage in Ockendon Road which is still there, and it's where my father and his brothers and sisters were born. I think they rented the cottage from the Gay family, who owned North Ockendon Hall. In 1926 Grandfather bought some land and had a house built in Fen Lane which he called Roselea and, at the side, there was a big enough yard to keep the thrashing machinery in.

The family business started in about 1870 – years before the advent of combine harvesters. Originally they used to cut the corn by scythe, then progressed to using a reaper. In those days, when the corn had been cut, it was tied into a sheaf by hand, with a tie being made by winding two lengths of straw taken from the crop. The sheaves were made into stacks, ready for the contractors to come along with the thrashing machine. Before the thrashing machine was invented, the corn was knocked out of the ears with a flail.

Ted and Louise White outside Blackbird Cottage, around 1920.

Steve White's grandfather with his thrashing gang, around 1920.

Steve White (right) at Barleylands Farm with his steam traction engine and thrasher.

A steam engine would drive the thrasher, and this hasn't changed much over the years. When the corn is stacked in the stack yard, the contractor stands the machine along the side of the stack, which then thrashes it to get the corn seed out. The straw would be used for animal bedding, feed, and thatching for roofs, amongst other things.

The sheaves from the stack would be forked on to the top of the thrashing machine, where the drum feeder would cut the string round the sheaf and feed it into the drum. The drum knocks out most of the ears from the crop being thrashed, which fall underneath the drum on to the sieves. The straw is thrown round from the drum onto the straw walkers, which move the straw out of the machine on to either a baler, a straw tier or chaff cutter, depending on what the farmer requires. The corn, chaff, short bits of straw and weed seeds go through different sieves, depending on the crop being thrashed.

The clean grain would pass through a rotary screen to grade the crop, i.e. into best corn, tail and weed seeds, then drop through corn spouts into bags, which would be taken back to the farm and out into the granary. The farmer might want the straw cut into chaff, which he could use for mixing with horse or cattle feed.

A bag of wheat would weigh eighteen stone, with barley weighing sixteen stone. Oats weighed twelve stone and beans, twenty-one stone. These bags would be carried on a man's back and put into the shed!

Tractors took over from the steam engines in about 1947 and prior to the steam engine being used, the thrashing machinery would have been pulled by shire horses.

We were the only thrashers in North Ockendon and the machines have changed little since about 1880. My grandfather had two sets of machinery, which were operated by the family. The thrashers needed to be at the farm at about half-past six in the morning, so they had a very early start. They'd cycle to work and not get home until seven in the evening. The machinery would be out all day and every day in my father's time.

Other thrashing outfits in the surrounding areas were Coles of Tilbury and Orsett, and Keeling's of Crays Hill, Billericay, and Randall's of Romford to name but a few; and we never encroached on other people's territory.

My grandfather didn't farm until 1953, as until then thrashing had been a full-time business, but in the late '40s and early '50s, combine harvesters began to come in. Although it took about ten or eleven years to completely finish the need for thrashers, the family had to do something else.

When Fairplay farm came up for sale in 1953, my grandfather bought it and had two semi-detached houses built nearby for his four sons. I've since combined the two houses, where I live with my family, and still work the farm where I grow wheat, barley, beans, etc. plus oilseed rape, which I sell mainly to merchants. There's still a good market for wheat as it's used for making bread and animal feed, etc. and oilseed rape is used for cooking. Barley is used for malting and animal feed.

Steve White

The Shepherd

Dad was a shepherd and we moved house fourteen times before I left school. He was an Essex man and in those days, when you worked for a farm, you nearly always lived in a tied cottage. He was an experienced shepherd, as was his father before him, and if he thought something wasn't being done properly, he'd argue with the boss. If they couldn't agree, he'd leave the job and we had to get out of the house with all our belongings being put out on to the village green.

It was when this happened on a South Ockendon farm that the council found us the house where I still live. I was about eleven at the time and I think this house was built on the orchards in the 1950s. There were kissing gates as entry to the orchards as they needed to get the horses through.

Brambles are taboo where sheep are concerned and on one occasion the farmer told Dad he wanted the sheep put into a certain meadow. Dad said it would be unwise as there was a thunderstorm coming, and if it caused the

High Street, South Ockendon, around the 1900s. (Courtesy of Brian Evans)

sheep to panic, they'd run into the brambles. But the farmer insisted on having his own way and at three o'clock in the morning he came knocking on our door because the sheep had panicked and were in the brambles. Dad said, 'You wanted them in there so you'd better get them out,' and we were on the move again. Everything we had was in a tea chest, with the breakables being wrapped in newspaper.

The family went to a farm in Crowborough from there. Mum was pregnant with me at the time and I was born in a little village called Withyham. If Dad wasn't able to find a job, we'd go to Mum's people in Dorset until Dad was in work again. He'd look for a position in the weekly *Farmer & Stockbreeder*. I used to go out with Dad quite a bit and run with the dogs and the sheep. I'd set aside an area of field and put little pens on it which I'd line with bales of straw so it was nice and warm. Then I'd collect the newly born lambs in a wheelbarrow and the old ewe would follow me. I'd put the lambs in a small pen and they'd stay there for three days before they were let out into the big wired pen. They'd always go back to their mother. We had a caravan with four wheels and that was our shepherd hut – we even had a little fire in it.

At one time Dad worked for Lord Rayleigh at Hatfield Peverel and all farms had a barn where the sheep were sheared. I recall one man being 'on the handle' all day long. The handle was on a machine that drove the clippers. I remember that, at the end of a shearing day, Dad could get a knife and cut the fat that had come from the wool from his sleeve. I'd be out with my father and the sheep all day during the summer holidays. A shepherd could do everything regarding looking after the flock. Sheep get 'fly', which is where a blowfly lays its maggots. If you don't keep the sheep clean, then in the end the maggots will kill the sheep. If the sheep cut themselves or get in the brambles, the next thing you know they've got maggots in their wool. Dad would give me the clippers and set me to checking the lambs for fly, and woe betide me if I missed one.

One farmer I worked for put a few sheep on the marshes. The governor was an agricultural farmer but it's what he wanted to do and when we went out there to check the sheep, I had to tell him one or two had fly. The governor asked me what I meant, so I showed him and we referred it back to Dad. The sheep had to be rubbed with a solution but my father would never divulge what it was, although I know it involved two chemicals. We also used to check the sheep's feet because if they get something between their toes then it festers.

Another job Dad had was in West Tisted in Hampshire. There were no sheep on the farm so he drove one of the first combine harvesters.

If you were showing a sheep, you'd trim the fleece so it had a square back. At one show his three ewes won a prize for the farmer my Dad worked for. A man approached him and offered him a job in New Zealand, but Dad wouldn't go. The last job he had was in Ockendon.

When the sheep died out round here he became a cow man. He used to milk the cows by hand at first. In those days you'd hand-wash the udders and sit on a little stool before milking. The milk would go out into a cooler before being churned. Lord Rayleigh had a big milk business.

We spent the war in Hatfield Peverel but later came back to South Ockendon and he finished up working on the buses. I think I can say that Dad was a bit short-tempered.

Vic Rampling

Research Project

When I was fifteen years old I was living in Germany. It was 1945 and my dream was to get into forestry, but there were no openings in schools at that time due to the political situation. I investigated training for all sorts of horticulture but, back then, food was considered more important than flowers, so my father suggested I find work.

He found a large fruit and vegetable farm which also produced fruit juice and I was able to get a three-year apprenticeship there. Having passed my exams, I found employment in another nursery, which grew tropical and other pot plants. After that, I added to my experience by taking over a small flower nursery where the previous owner had died.

Having worked in Sweden, where I'd gained some forestry experience, I found employment in Switzerland and was planning to work in Holland where I would have needed to speak English. Unfortunately my English wasn't of a good enough standard, so I came to England to improve it.

I found a job in Whetstone and, in 1955, arrived at the Swan Lane Nursery in North London. The money was poor – paying only £6 per week – but food was provided, along with a room in the manager's house. I only stayed for four months before finding a job in Camden Town which paid £12 per week. This seemed better but unfortunately they didn't tell me how many hours I'd have to work, which proved to be excessive. The business provided flower decorations to London's big hotels, plus displays for big events such as the Farnborough Air Show and Olympia etc. My job included running their small nursery in Camden Place and I was provided with a lorry and driver. We'd go round to all the big nurseries

Greenhouses at Hall Farm, 1960s.

where I'd select flowers and plants for the displays and I won many silver and gold medals for my work.

On the way to England I'd met the lady who later became my wife. When she was expecting our first child we needed more room, so I found another job in a small nursery in Shirley, Croydon. We stayed there for seven years and now had two children. I didn't seem to be getting any further with my career, so finally, although we liked living in England, we decided to go back to Germany.

I advertised for a job in a high-class German horticultural nursery paper, giving my credentials and qualifications plus detailing my experience, and gave my English address. I received four or five offers from Germany but was undecided what to do when I unexpectedly had an offer to act as manager of a greenhouse area in North Ockendon. I accepted the offer and was interviewed on site by the investors. Although they were directors of Shand Kydd Wallpapers and Polycell, the project, called Edgeware Agricultural Research, was a private investment.

Katya, my wife, was unsure about relocating into the country as she was a town girl, but we moved into a half-ready cottage at No. 6, Church Lane.

In the first year we bought all the plants from Lincolnshire but during the winter of 1963 we had five months of very cold weather which more or less destroyed the crop. The greenhouses failed and the water was frozen. At harvest time we had about forty Spaniards and Irish here – they were on piecework but, with nobody confirming their output, they walked away with double what they'd really earned.

Another man, Bob Hill, who arrived three months after me, had run big fields in Lincolnshire so he took over all the 120 acres of fields, leaving me to grow my plants. I had one and a half acres of mobile glasshouses and two propagating houses. I brought in hyacinths etc., and Bob Hill sorted out the labour so the wage bill more or less halved. The project was beginning to bring in a bit of money in so the people in London were happy. The man who ran the show had always bought the compost we used from John Innes, but I began making my own peat-based growing medium, which saved a little more money.

We continued in this way for a couple of years until Mr T.J. Billings put in an offer for the business. The directors decided to sell to him and in 1965 he bought the 120 acres to graze his dairy herd. The herd was in Kent at the time but the land there was divided by roads, whereas in North Ockendon the fields were continuous. Unfortunately we were blighted by foot-and-mouth disease in 1967 so the herd was unable to move over to North Ockendon for three or four years. Eventually we had 100 milkers here and some young animals.

The man who'd been in charge of the project left, and since Mr Billings was a farmer he gave me full control of the nurseries. I used the two small greenhouses with staging for pot plants and grew many other varieties. We forced lily of the valley which was very successful for the wedding market, and that lasted for about twenty years.

Mr Billings sold the farm in 1983, and I bought seventeen acres of the total farm so we could continue to run the nursery. I had a foreman who learned about winemaking at his college and he suggested we try to produce some here. I was apprehensive but we had a quarter-acre of walled garden so we bought the vines from Germany and started to make our own wine. Although the quality was acceptable I didn't find it of particular interest, so we didn't pursue it.

My main interest was in chrysanthemums – and I grew a large variety. The old cowshed was full of them. The blooms are very tender – one touch and the petals could fall. The boiler we were using to heat the nursery was far too big so we either had to get a smaller boiler or build another half-acre of glass. At that time crude oil cost just eight pence per gallon so I persuaded Mr Billings to build the other half-acre. Chrysanthemums are a short-day plant so we had to black out all the nurseries – if the plants get too much light they keep on growing and will never flower, so we didn't want that. By shortening the day length we could produce flowers that bloomed all year round and in that way we maintained an all-year crop. I was able to tell the different varieties by their leaf.

People liked big chrysanthemums for Christmas – the large incurves were very popular and it was a big market for us. We had to be precise and get the plants to bloom on 19 and 20 December, so we switched off the lights in the greenhouses

Chrysanthemums in the greenhouses, 1960s.

just twelve weeks before Christmas. Later, the spray variety began to get more popular. They're easier to grow because all that's needed is to take the top bud out, then the sides will grow. With the blooms, however, all the side buds need to be removed, which is time-consuming.

The winter storms of 1987 almost destroyed the nursery and felled some of the trees but we managed to save some. During another winter we lost a greenhouse and I used the insurance money to buy three plastic tunnels and we grew carnations for a while.

Hall Farm was the biggest in the village at one time, with Manor Farm being the second largest, then White Post. The old farmhouse was bombed during the Second World War and the remains are under our front lawn.

When I retired I handed control over to my son, Martin, who'd now finished studying Agricultural Botany at Bangor University.

Reiner Hegmann

Seven

PROFESSIONS
AND OCCUPATIONS

Warley Hospital

When my mother worked in Warley Hospital, they arranged for a bus to pick up
employees who lived in Ockendon, Belhus and Aveley. At the same time, I was
training at Warley but I lived in their student accommodation. I'd trained as a
general nurse in Orsett Hospital and I've always worked in the community since
the mid-1980s, but since I retired I only do two days per week.

Margaret Abboyi

Memorial tablet in South Ockendon Hospital Memorial Garden.

Shirt Factory

I was born in Cliff Place, near to the village church. When I left school I worked at the shirt factory, which was on the main road towards Brentwood. It was run by the Co-op and we made shirts, pyjamas and nightshirts and we'd alternate between working on the feeders and belts. We'd sit round the fountain to eat our lunch in summer, listening to the peacocks screeching. I loved it there but when the time-and-motion people came in everything changed, and not for the better. When the factory eventually closed down we all cried. There was a Co-op drinks factory further along the road. Then I went to Gordon's factory, where we made dresses. In those days we could walk through the kissing gates and over the railway line and into Ardmore Road.

Yvonne Rampling

Midwife

When I left school I trained as a general nurse in King George's Hospital which was then near Ley Street in Ilford. It was also near the railway and during the war they had a gun on that line – it used to go up and down all night trying to shoot the planes down. We didn't see much of the war in Basildon – just the planes going over during the Blitz. I loved my training at King George's and fortunately there were some friends with me from back in my schooldays.

In 1939, I left King George's to do my midwifery training at Leytonstone Hospital. We trainee midwives had to go out in the middle of the night on a bicycle – there were no street lights allowed – but we got to know the policemen on their beats and felt quite safe. When a call was received from a mother-to-be, the trainee was the first on the scene and it was our responsibility to call for the midwife at the last minute, when we felt she was needed.

I still worked for a short time when I married as my husband and I lived with my parents for a while, so I used to help the local midwife, who was also the district nurse in Basildon.

Evelyn Cressey

Evening Work

When I was married I could only work during the evenings, so did a 5–8 shift at the South Ockendon hospital as a domestic. The hospital grounds were beautifully

Memorial Garden in Brandon Groves.

laid out and well cared for. The patients were mentally disabled and I'd be sent to a different ward each day. I had a few disturbing experiences but it was when a particular incident occurred that I decided it was time to leave. Thank goodness there's a different attitude towards care of the mentally disabled these days.

Maria Proctor

Hairdressing

I left Gaynes School in 1942 when I was fourteen, and was apprenticed to a hairdressing salon in Romford. I earned 5*s* per week so when the 4*d* was deducted for my National Insurance stamp, I took home just 4*s* 8*d*.

Gwen Bishop

Marley Tiles

Dad worked at Marley Tiles and they manufactured roof tiles there. The building was in Stifford Road, which is between Daiglen Drive and Foyle Drive.

The employees were well looked after, with various football pitches and a clubhouse. He also worked at Tilbury power station and if he was kept late he'd walk all the way home to South Ockendon.

Adrian Inglefield

Ling's

John Ling, my grandfather on my mother's side, came down to South Ockendon in 1896. He'd served his apprenticeship as a farrier in Ringsfield in Suffolk where he was born and, when he arrived, he began working for Mr Pruce, the blacksmith. He was always looking for an opportunity to work for himself so started to mend bicycles at night and do other odd jobs, until eventually he was able to open his own little bike shop. That shop was called J. Ling and it's still there, although it's run as an insurance business now.

Pear Tree House was a big Georgian house just as you turned into West Road – it's since been pulled down. As you turned into North Road there was a coach house and stables belonging to Pear Tree House, which was where the doctor lived. Immediately after that were two little shops, one of which was my grandfather's. He mended and sold bicycles and anything else he could turn his hand to. That would have been in the early 1900s and he moved from there later. He died in 1918 and my grandmother held on to the business and one of my uncles helped her run it. My uncle needed to be released from his apprenticeship at County Motor Works in Chelmsford so he could help her and, when grandmother approached the company, they agreed. They also said that, should she wish it, they'd be happy to take the next son when he became of age and that is what happened. They eventually moved premises and changed the name to M. Ling & Sons. There was a yard at the back of the shop and from there they repaired cars, vans, lorries and tractors. The two boys ran the business until they shut up shop in the 1960s, when the LCC took over the leases.

John Litton

Schoolteacher

I taught at Benyon Infants School in South Ockendon for two years from 1960 to 1962, but I was an uncertified teacher so left there to go to college. Initially I'd gone to the education office which was in Hall Lane, Upminster for a job as a childminder. I was told my qualifications were such that they wanted me as a teacher

Pupils at Benyon School, early '6os.

and gave me the option of teaching infants, junior or secondary children. I decided on infants and by half-past three that afternoon had a job at Hacton Infants School in Hornchurch. I had one day's observation with a class of forty-eight pupils before I started work! I taught at three schools, one of which was Benyon, and I remember the inspectors coming to encourage me to apply for college.

I went to college in Brentwood in 1962 to gain my teaching qualifications and, as I was over twenty-six by then, did the mature student course and went on from there to teach all over Essex. I ended up as a head teacher. In 1959, teachers were still very thin on the ground. After the war there'd been a shortage of teachers and members of the armed forces were encouraged to take five terms of teacher training without a break, to swell the dwindling numbers.

The head teacher at Benyon was Mrs Taylor and she held brief over the infants school. This was a modern building with six or seven classrooms and was situated behind the junior school. My five-year-old daughter came with me and she remembers a pointillism picture in the vestibule. One morning, after assembly, her class was shown this picture and they too attempted to paint in the same style.

The gardens were very attractive with a large weeping willow.

The junior school was headed by Mr Impey. He always seemed imposing to me as he was very tall. The only time we had contact with the junior school was when we went over to have lunch – I don't remember there being kitchens in our school. The junior school was very old, probably Victorian, but I didn't go inside as a large hut at the rear was used as the dining room. It had shiny red floors.

On one occasion (we didn't have the luxury of teaching assistants in those days), a child came to ask if he could go to the toilet. I was sharpening pencils with my head over the waste-paper basket as I said, 'yes', but he still stayed beside me. He asked again and this time I looked up and said, 'yes' once more. He went off quite unperturbed but I wondered why he'd not gone the first time. I queried whether he might be deaf and a few weeks later he became the proud owner of a rather cumbersome hearing aid. By this time he was six, and nobody had realised he was deaf. The rest of the class wanted to be like him and made hearing aids out of plasticine. I loved the way the children supported him by making him feel special.

I'd moved to Hullbridge from Hornchuch at the start of my second year and had to take a bus to Rayleigh station, a train to Brentwood and another bus to South Ockendon. My travelling companion was Elsie Mason, who was an inspiration to me. Three other teachers I remember were Miss Dollamore, Mrs Ping and Mrs Parry, who was the deputy head.

The school overlooked fields, and pigs were kept in an adjacent enclosure. My daughter recalls when a bull was loose in the village and everyone stayed inside until he was caught. Our class had a pet tortoise who we named Jet as he could travel at an alarming speed. We also had a gerbil who escaped one weekend.

Susan Collier and Madeline Pound at Walton-on-the-Naze.

We found her in a box of scraps but unfortunately she'd damaged her eye and had to be taken to the vet to have it removed. It did not deter her wanderlust.

There was a home for people with cerebral palsy in the village and at Easter we collected Easter eggs and decorated big cardboard boxes which were sent to the people who lived there.

While we waited for the bus in the evening, we'd go across to the bakery and buy their delicious fresh bread. South Ockendon was a sleepy village in those days, built around the green and the village church.

When I left the school I was given a beautiful string of pearls. In the following weeks the family went to Walton-on-the-Naze for a holiday and I was surprised to find one of the pupils I'd left behind, Susan Collier, at the same caravan park. She and my daughter had a grand time together and we'd often take her out with us. I took a picture of the two girls on the camp quad bikes.

Jean Pound

Chemists and Greyhounds

When I left school at fifteen I joined a work experience scheme in the area and my first job was with Hements, the chemists in Daiglen Drive – I really liked it there and they involved me in several of the procedures, but it was only temporary. After that I went to the kennels in North Road. The dogs were mostly retired greyhounds but they boarded domestic dogs as well and I used to help clean the kennels and walk the dogs.

Later I worked full time in the Ockendon Crèche as a trainee nursery assistant, but the crèche has gone now.

Maria Proctor

Bata Shoe Factory

At one time Mum worked at the Bata Shoe Factory in East Tilbury – they ran a bus from outlying areas to get their people to work. She also worked in South Ockendon Hospital. I can't remember much about it as I was young at the time, but I recall her coming home in her blue uniform, although she wasn't a nurse. She didn't stay in that job for long as said she didn't like it very much.

Adrian Inglefield

Hairdressing in Hornchurch

I was apprenticed to hairdressing when I left school and I used to cycle to and from Hornchurch among the shrapnel and incendiaries. This was about the only job I could get where I didn't have to travel to London, but later I opened my own shops.

Peter Coe

Speedway Racing

When I came out of the air force I had no trade so found it difficult to get a job, but eventually went into speedway racing. My brother and I had never been on a motorbike but he wrote away for trials and we were given a job. I rode for a team called Rayleigh Rockets in Southend, where I rubbed shoulders with the likes of ace riders such as Howdy Byford, Eric Chitty, Malcolm Craven, and Cliff Watson. In those days Split Waterman was the star rider at Wembley. The manager signed my brother first and he developed a very good reputation as a fast and clean rider.

Jim McGillivray, the speedway rider.

We performed on Saturday nights at Rayleigh Stadium but I was never as good a rider as my brother, so when I was offered a job at the Co-op Dairy in Romford, I took it and stayed there for thirty-two years.

Jim McGillivray

The Forge

The Forge, which was run by Harry Cressey and had been in his family for generations, was at the centre of village farming life. All the local farmers used Harry's expertise with metal repairs, tool making etc., and of course for the shoeing of all the horses in the area. On a wet day you could always guarantee finding several farmers gathered there with bits and pieces for repair of almost anything used on a farm. I can remember taking our gramophone with a broken spring to him, which was eventually mended. Looking back, the workshop was quite an example of days gone by. The main forge was hand pumped by large bellows and all the major tools, such as the drilling machine, were hand operated. Before the advent of acetylene welding, metal was heated up in the roaring fire and then beaten together on the anvil to form a weld.

Horseshoes were made from scratch, which was an art in its own right. The smell of hot shoes being placed on a horse's hoof, to get the correct fit, is something one will never forget. They were afterwards quenched in the small tank of water on the front of the anvil before being nailed to the hoof. The main entry for the horses into the forge building was from the main road.

Two horses at a time could be accommodated and I can still visualise Mr Cressey in his long leather apron which protected him from flying sparks when working with red hot metal. He'd lift a horse's foot between his legs, trimming the hoof with a large, very sharp knife which he had made from an old sword. Several swords were kept for this purpose in the rafters. Following the war his son, John, joined him and carried on the business with him until his father's death, then Roger Bonnett joined John in a new partnership named Cressey & Bonnett. They built the new workshops and the historic old forge became redundant, so was used as a garage by John's brother-in-law, Tarry Shaw. The main front doors were boarded up and the west end wall of the old workshop was removed to allow the car to enter.

Geoff Jones

The Blacksmith

Jobs were scarce after the war so, although he wasn't really built for it, my husband became a blacksmith like his father. When we were shoeing the horses the men would go to their farms on bikes, then bring back any horse to us that needed shoeing. They'd leave it with us while they had breakfast and pick it up later.

Old Mr Cressey died in 1955. My husband continued to do the shoeing and other things for a while but after the war the farms gradually became mechanised and all the horses went. When the horses finished we began servicing tractors – we had to move with the times. We established the workshop in the grounds of the old forge in 1957, and then moved into the new workshop ten years later.

Evelyn Cressey

Benyon Estate Office

My grandfather on my father's side went to work for the Benyon estate in 1909. The house, which was the headquarters for maintaining the estate's properties etc., is on the opposite side of the road to Bridge Cottages. Grandfather built sheds all the way down the sides of the yard, of which the two end ones were

Benyon estate house.

used for drying timber. They'd cut the timber down on the estate and bring it into the sheds, where it was put up on pegs and left to dry. The middle of the shed was used as the workshop – with the large space in the centre being the carpenters' shop – and the smaller sections used for lime and wallpaper. At the further end, paint was stored. My mother's people were from South Ockendon and my father's people came from Devon. Dad was in the Royal Navy and based at Portsmouth – he was a ship's carpenter.

From time to time, Squire Benyon came down to Upminster by train. He'd walk across the fields and stay in the estate house or in Holly Lodge and the land agent, Captain Paul, would do the same. My grandfather died when I was eighteen months old so I don't remember him, but I was told that when he came down here he used to drive around in his pony and trap. He'd use it to take my grandmother to do her shopping in Grays. Bob Day, who was the general handyman for the estate, also used to drive to Grays. When the First World War began, the government commandeered my grandfather's pony.

Squire Benyon was a descendant of Lord Salisbury and the Benyon family still live on their Englefield estate in Berkshire. When the Benyons sold up in 1936, Surridges bought the estate house. Fred Surridge also bought Manor Farm, which was run by Mr Fisher. At the same time, George Gunary & Sons bought Hall and White Post Farms.

Eventually my brother and I were given the option to buy the old estate house, as we'd been running our plant-hire business from there for some time. When I retired in 2003 we sold the house, which is now in private hands.

We kept the orchard and a bit of glebe land we'd bought from the church. Later we took the council up on their offer to plant trees on it. They said they'd supply the labour and we could buy the trees, which at least keeps the land safe from development, etc.

These houses, Nos 1 and 2, Bridge Cottages, were built by the Benyons for key men who worked for the yard and the remainder on this side of the road were all farm cottages. I remember the abundance of lilac that grew over the gates back then. When the estate was broken up, my father bought our two cottages for £450 for the pair. Mr Benyon owned a lot of property around here. Miss Stokes lived next door and her brother, Jimmy, worked over the road as a carpenter.

John Litton

Slaughter Family

Dad was chauffeur/gardener to the Slaughter family, who owned a ladder company in the Plaistow area. The Slaughters lived in Hutton Mount and my father worked part-time for them until the end of the war, when he started up on his own. He swept chimneys and cleaned windows and, at the same time, kept pigs on this site.

I've always said that after the war you could walk from Grays war memorial to Purfleet and pick up any job you wanted. With all the industry in the area in those days, there was full employment.

Eric Jiggens

Eight

PLACES AND PEOPLE
OF INTEREST

Litte Belhus House

When my wife and I moved into Little Belhus House, our optimism faded a little as we realised the enormity of the task we'd taken on. The house smelled of dust and neglect, while birds fluttered through broken windowpanes. But we loved its character and history. So began a restoration project that lasted for ten years; although with a house dating back to at least 1603, maintenance is ongoing.

We spent every evening and weekend for the next seven years working on the house. One area at a time was restored, making sure everything was in keeping with its age, and I was determined that 'everything that came out, went back'. The exceptions are the modern kitchen and bathrooms.

We've researched the property a lot but don't know if the house was in the grounds when the original Belhus estate was developed or whether it was encompassed within the estate at a later date. There's evidence of the latter, as some of Little Belhus seems to be much older than the mansion and is thought to have been used as a hunting lodge. We know there was a footpath from here that led directly to the mansion. Folklore has it that Queen Elizabeth I used to have dalliances here – it's also claimed she spent the night in the house when she came to address her troops at Tilbury.

We also know the Manning family had the house for a long time – they were tenant farmers and there used to be huge barns in the immediate area.

London County Council bought much of the Belhus estate and surrounding farmland in the 1930s, and the mansion and park were occupied by the army during the Second World War, but the house was neglected and eventually had to be knocked down.

Little Belhus House.

James I plaque, Little Belhus House.

Little Belhus House survived and, when the council took it over, they rebuilt the roof and restored the house to quite a high standard so they could rent it out. It's said they even furnished the house with antiques before it was let to professional people.

Later they converted the house into three dwellings and used it for social housing but, when the residents left, the house was sold privately as two houses. The smaller lodge is still attached to Little Belhus House.

The house is Grade II* listed and on the wall of the porch is a plaque representing a coat of arms given by James I to a local knight (possibly one of the Barrett-Lennards) in the seventeenth century. It depicts a lion and unicorn, with his royal crest in the centre, and unifies England and Scotland represented by the Tudor rose and thistle. I resited this from a wall in the garden as I felt it had been exposed to the elements for long enough.

The front door is original and of solid wood, obviously aged and extremely heavy. My first job was to completely rebuild the thirteen mullioned and transomed windows. I restored all the wood, alternating between scaffolding towers at the front and rear. This enabled Tina, my wife, to paint the renewed windows, keeping them free from wood dust. We used to laugh and say we only saw each other at weekends.

The timber-framed house is Elizabethan, while much of the restoration work is Georgian. The house underwent a transformation in Georgian times and most of the doors and floorboards are of that period, although the floorboards in one of the bedrooms are thought to be original. We took up each Georgian floorboard and sanded it by hand. There are some fine examples of oak panelling in several of the rooms.

At some point the house was galleried but now has new ceilings, albeit some of them are of reed, and the rooms are light and airy. We used breathable paint to help preserve the walls, and there is some insulation between the plasterboard. There is some lath and plaster.

We made sure every part of the restoration has been accomplished on a like-for-like basis, with replacement timber being sourced from the Belhus estate. I opened up the flu in the dining room and made the fireplace, its only decoration being a Tudor rose which I made from a mould of an original in a bedroom. The drawing room is panelled.

The sixteenth-century friezes over the fireplace in the lounge and the master bedroom are replicas of those to be found in Porters – the mayor's residence in Southend – and Eastbury Manor in Barking, which is a National Trust property. The fireplaces were designed by the same person and there are only four known examples in Essex, with Little Belhus having two of them.

Interior example of Little Belhus House.

We've kept the furnishings in keeping with the age and ambience of the house and there's a cabinet in the oak-panelled drawing room which displays some artefacts I dug up in the garden. There are some very old glass bottles, a flint Stone-Age tool, a halfpenny dated 1775 and some old clay pipes.

Naturally the woodwork in a house of this age sports carpenters' signatures, plus notches on the woodwork, thought to be vital in medieval times to ward off witches.

Thurrock Council Heritage monitored the progress of the restoration and were impressed enough to issue us with letters of commendation.

The house is surrounded by half an acre of walled gardens, so we are completely private. To the rear, there is a mulberry tree which is at least 400 years old. Several stately homes around the country are known to have such trees, as King James I imported them from China with a view to building a silk industry. It is said the Chinese took his money but sent us black mulberries, whereas those needed to feed silkworms are white.

The exterior of the house is weatherboarded and we also have a bell tower. The bell, dating back to 1763, is thought to have come from South Ockendon church when the latter obtained a replacement.

Peter King

Domestic Service

My mother, Blanche Rydings (*née* Turner), was in service at Little Belhus House from 1916 to 1919. Although she was married, she continued to work while my father was serving in the First World War. They met by the ferry at Tilbury, where he was stationed. Mother had taken the ferry from Gravesend where she was in service and dropped the bag of plums she was carrying. Dad picked them up for her and always joked that not only did he pick up her plums – he picked her up too!

At one point Mum's father was farm bailiff at Great Garlands Farm but the family later moved to Stifford and she'd go by foot from there to South Ockendon. Walking through the adjoining fields, she'd pass Quince Tree Cottage opposite the hospital, then into more open ground to Little Belhus House.

Her sister, Elsie, worked with her too and one night during a Zeppelin air raid, a large globe of the world which stood at the top of the staircase toppled as the

Blanche Rydings
(*née* Turner) in Little
Belhus House gardens,
around 1917.

Blanche and Elsie Turner at Great Garlands Farm, with their father, early 1900s.

house shook from falling bombs. Elsie, who was only about fourteen at the time, ran around the house shouting, 'the world has fallen over'!

She also told how rats would run along the rafters in the attics where they slept.

There was an army officer who lived in the Belhus mansion at the time, and he offered to look for a nice gift for my father's birthday. He bought a lovely cut-throat razor which Mum gave to Dad, but sadly it was stolen from his kitbag during the war.

My mother worked at Little Belhus House for the duration of the war but left when my father came home from the army.

Ken Rydings

Mary Magdelene Church, North Ockendon

I held my first service in St Mary Magdalene church, North Ockendon in December 1978.

The incumbent 'rector,' the Revd Kenneth Briggs, had died that December so the church was without a priest. I went along to take the Christmas services and continued to help out.

Revd Briggs, who was semi-retired and helping out at North Ockendon alongside the Revd Steel, had his own house in Emerson Park so the rectory had been sold in 1976. The Diocese of Chelmsford suspended the living of North Ockendon, so the parish had no stipend or house to offer a clergyman.

St Mary Magdalene church, North Ockendon.

Poyntz Memorial in St Mary Magdalene church.

I'd been an industrial chaplain in the East End but the industrial chaplains at the Diocese of London decided that, with the closure of the upper docks, there was really no longer the need for one. I was transferred to Chelmsford, in order to retain my stipend, expenses and housing, and eventually it was decided I would do half a day a week and conduct the Sunday services in North Ockendon, whilst carrying on with my own job as industrial chaplain in the Port of London.

The local church community were consulted and some were unhappy at not having a full-time priest, but I was appointed priest-in-charge and carried on with my industrial chaplaincy while I lived in Upminster.

Stained-glass window, St Mary Magdalene church.

The brown-brick rectory, which was rebuilt in 1750, suffered bomb damage in 1944 and in 1958 the top storey of the north wing was taken down while the rest of the floor was converted into a separate flat. The Diocesan Authorities sold the rectory into private hands in 1975.

The church has always been well supported by the local population, as it's at the heart of the community. In the summer we hold a fête on the rectory meadow, where we have stalls, sideshows, raffles, competitions, etc. and of course, the usual refreshments. We used to have a drama group called The Poyntz Players, and held concerts in the church hall. These events were always packed.

The church school had been rebuilt in 1902 by James Benyon for eighty children but gradually numbers dwindled. When I first went there the school was still in operation for primary and junior pupils, so we had to use the Reading Room for concerts etc. But in 1980, when the number of pupils had dwindled to just sixteen, the government decided it was no longer financially viable and the school closed. The children transferred mainly to Oglethorpe in Cranham, or to Branfil in Upminster.

The Benyon family, who built North Ockendon Church School, were from South Ockendon and fortunately in the deeds it stipulated that, if the school ceased to be used as such, then it was to become the rooms for the

North Ockendon church. So, when the school closed, the building wasn't appropriated by the government and it became our church hall.

We installed some toilets because the schoolchildren had used outside facilities, although there was one inside toilet provided for the staff. There was a kitchen etc. and the church paid for the upkeep. So the school was upgraded and, when it closed, we created a youth club which has now gone as there are hardly any children remaining in the village.

After the closure of the school another organisation was set up called The Good Companions but that's now gone as it ran out of members – people got too old, etc. The Men's Fellowship ceased too.

We rely on special occasions and monthly coffee mornings for people to come together now and the proceeds are donated to charity. We have bring-and-buy, and a raffle etc. and we usually raise between £200 and £300 each time.

At one point, North Ockendon was still vibrant, while South Ockendon was a bit slow, so their Brownies came over to us, and they still come along to the family service once a month.

The old school was set apart from the church. This was awkward for Sunday school pupils in the winter as the children had to traipse from the hall, along Church Lane, and into the church for services. So the school was sold and converted into flats and we used the money from that to build a new hall beside the church. It has a modern kitchen, toilets, handicapped access and handicapped toilets, etc.

At one time while I was serving, the official population of the village was approximately 150 while the electoral roll stated 130. Records show that the population was 351 in 1891 and this declined to 291 in 1931. As far as the attendees of the church are concerned, they come from all around Hornchurch, South Ockendon, Upminster, and Grays.

I left North Ockendon in 1993 and was appointed to relate to the development of the Thames Gateway. Because of my links with the India/Millwall and Royal Docks etc. they wanted me to do that in addition to the port chaplaincy, so I was removed from North Ockendon.

But there was a long interregnum (which is the period between priests) and that went on for about eighteen months, so I was still taking the services at North Ockendon, although a few other clergymen were helping out. Then they appointed a new priest, and he was there until he died four years later, so there was another interregnum and I got called in yet again. I was still associated with the church and helped out with services during holidays etc. and there was yet another interregnum and I was called out again until the new clergyman was appointed. He left last November and I'm helping out once more, so I've

Interior of St Mary Magdalene church.

had four interregnums since I first began in North Ockendon in 1978, and I've worked there on and off since. That's about thirty-five years. The original church of St Mary Magdalene, which existed as early as 1075, was attached to Westminster Abbey's manor of North Ockendon. Architecturally, it's made up of the chancel, with a north vestry and Lady Chapel, a nave with a north aisle, a south porch and a west tower. Its walls are of flint and rag-stone and 'dressed' with Reigate stone. Various enhancements have been made over the centuries and an organ gallery was built in 1840. Richard Benyon funded the cost of the complete restoration carried out in 1858.

The church has six bells and we have a very good team of bellringers, who've won competitions in Essex. Four of the bells were cast by Miles Graye in 1621, and the fifth in 1695 by Philip Wightman with the treble added in 1934, having been cast by Mills and Stainbank.

There are some impressive monuments and brasses inside the church, which relate to dignitaries associated with North Ockendon.

Canon Frank Hackett

Ground Knuts

Years ago the churchyard at St Mary Magdalene became very overgrown with cow parsley covering the grass, which in the summertime reached four feet or so in height. Usually the church wardens, Luther William from Upminster, and Leslie Cole, who farmed Puddledock Farm at the end of Clay Tye Road, would arrange for a group of men, who were church members, to spend an evening trying to tidy up. Everyone was expected to bring his own tools, so an array of scythes, bean hooks, rakes etc. would be assembled and they'd put in a hard evening's work.

One of the main problems was that the churchyard was covered by many headstones which made the task more difficult, so permission was sought to remove those erected before a certain date. Consent having been granted, they were initially laid against the wall of the farm buildings on the south side of the church. As far as I remember no note was made of the inscriptions, but it was assumed that the burial register would have details of who was buried where. Some stones were broken up and used on the path at the rear of the church, to what was then the vestry door.

The absence of the headstones made life a lot easier for clearing weeds and grass, and Leslie Cole could use his little Fordson Dexta Tractor, with a hay-mower fitted, to do the bulk of the work. This was all right until one year the front

Ground Knuts, 2003. From left: Malcolm Millard, Jim Wild, Geoff Jones, Graham Siblet, John King, Dennis Sorenson.

wheels of the tractor fell into a grave that had subsided and, even with the help of many hands, it took a long time to get it out.

Bill Garnham, who lived in South Ockendon and was a regular church and choir member at North Ockendon, worked for Thurrock Parks Department. He and his son Geoffrey took over the task of keeping the churchyard tidy for many years, in fact until he retired from work and moved to Frinton. As I had just retired in 1991, I volunteered to take over from Bill, and Jim Wild agreed to join me, so every Tuesday morning we met to do what we could, taking our own mowers and tools. We were soon joined by Graham Sibley and it was then that my wife Jan started calling us the 'ground nuts'. I remembered from schooldays that a Georgian term for an eligible young gentleman or dandy was a 'knut,' and so we adopted this and became the Ground Knuts.

Work became a regular thing on a Tuesday morning, holding the important executive meeting in the Old White Horse afterwards. We were well supported by the clergy, with all the ministers we've had over the years occasionally joining us at the Old White Horse following a morning's work. My wife Jan made us sweatshirts with a motif of two peanuts attired as gardeners with a mower and tools, stating, 'Ground Knuts try to do it most Tuesdays'.

We then decided that we needed a president for the group and the late Peter Cross agreed. On his demise, Tarry Shaw agreed to take his place. Since Tarry's death it has been agreed that no further president would be appointed as such, as it seems it could be fatal and not a good position to hold, although Arthur Driver now holds a similar position without the name.

Each week we each made a contribution towards the costs involved, such as petrol for mowers and beer at the executive meeting. Jim Wild was made treasurer, and things went so well that we were able to buy two new rotary mowers and hand tools with our accumulated funds. A large cylinder-type mower was donated by Alan Gibb of Ladyville Lodge, and David Scott arranged the purchase of a ship's container which was put at the west end of the churchyard as a shed/store. Dennis Sorenson joined us and, as a former pavier for the local council, became a great asset, repairing old tombs and graves.

Geoff Jones

Pumping the Organ

As a child I went to church in South Ockendon because that was where my Grandmother Scott lived, but later we went to North Ockendon church twice on Sunday and I was church warden there until I retired. I was baptised there, as were all my family, and it's still my church. We have fond memories of a chap called George who was a resident in South Ockendon Hospital. He worshipped at our church every Sunday and pumped the organ for us – he also insisted with dusting the pews. We were all upset when he passed away and had a plaque commemorating his life placed on the back on the organ.

Joy Scott

St Nicholas Church, South Ockendon

The church of St Nicholas, which stands on the south-east side of the village green, is noted for its circular west tower. When it was originally built, towers of this design were costly, which suggests South Ockendon was a wealthy parish. It's thought the height of the tower may have been reduced during rebuilding after it collapsed twice in the eighteenth century. The church is built from flint and rubble with ashlar dressings and only the west wall remains intact from the twelfth-century building.

Richard Benyon and Henry Eve funded a considerable restoration of St Nicholas in 1866. Henry Eve was rector at the time and they chose Richard Armstrong as the architect. At the same time the bell was replaced by one made by Mears and Stainbank.

St Nicholas church, South Ockendon.

A large marble Elizabethan wall monument is the defining feature of the Lady Chapel. It shows the kneeling figures of Sir Richard and Lady Susannah Saltonstall in full court dress. Sir Richard, who lived from 1521 to 1601, was a London merchant who bought the South Ockendon estate from Edward Tyrell in 1576. Sir Richard was a patron of the church, and later became Lord Mayor of London. He and Lady Susannah had about seventeen children, all of whom survived to adulthood, although one died as a teenager. The sons were modelled from real life, so it's an exceptional monument. There are other memorials of the descendants of Sir Richard, but none so grand as the wall monument.

A later addition to the church is the beautifully carved oak altar. This was donated from the chapel belonging to South Ockendon Hospital when it closed.

I was ordained twenty years ago in 1993. I wanted to go into the church when I was seventeen but it was thought I was too young, so I went to university, after which I worked as a teacher and social worker. My home was in Heston, West London – near Heathrow, in fact. I grew up with the noise of aircraft and, although one becomes inured to it when you live under a flight path, I might notice it when (or if) I return to visit.

When the last vicar retired in September 2012, we rejigged the parishes. St Nicholas (South Ockendon) and All Saints (Belhus Park) have been on United Benefice for about eleven years. The term 'United Benefice' is where two parishes are linked and, although they remain separate parishes, they share a vicar. We have also gone into a Team Ministry whereby St Nicholas (South Ockendon), All Saints (Belhus Park), St Michaels (Aveley), and St Stephens (Purfleet) are embraced within one large parish. So we are now four parishes within one big parish sharing three vicars.

When I had a parish in North London I was the sole incumbent and I found it very lonely. It was a hard job as I was responsible for everything and had no real support. Although some people enjoy being king in their own domain, personally, I found it isolating. Therefore, I find the new arrangement very satisfying and love having the support of my colleagues in the four parishes. For example, I no longer have the worry of finding a replacement when I go on holiday, or to a meeting, nor have I the sole responsibility of running courses, etc. so the new arrangement suits me very well. I still have my own little patch but I'm well supported by the rest of the team.

This system has only been in operation since 1 April 2013 so we're still learning how to do it as we have a new level of administration and hierarchy. So whereas before responsibility stopped with the church wardens, we now have four parishes involved.

The post of church warden is a voluntary one and the oldest elected position in the world, going back to the reign of Queen Elizabeth I.

Church wardens have responsibility for overseeing the buildings and finance of the parish with the incumbent, administration and ministry of the church. They have more or less a 'fixtures and fittings' and admin role – in other words,

'money and bricks'. We have regular meetings within a whole committee structure and I meet with my wardens frequently.

I've been involved with St Nicholas for about five years and, although we're in the centre of the village, it's on the edge of a community of about 20,000 people.

We had a large amount of work done on St Nicholas church in 2007/08 which took about three months to complete. We put in water and heating, which enabled us to install a kitchen and toilet. The church had had no running water for 800 years. We replaced old electric infrared heaters with gas central heating.

Saltonstall wall monument, St Nicholas church.

Part of that project was to put in wooden and glass panels to box in the south aisle where we've created a community room, which includes the toilet and kitchenette. It means the children can now use that space for Sunday school and afterwards we can have coffee there. It's been a slow process but we now have a 'knit and natter' group which comes in each Wednesday lunchtime. It's also a craft group and is arranged to fit in with school hours. Although it has about twenty members in all, at any one time a group of about eight people attend. During school holidays it acts as a craft group for children and recently I was French knitting with the children, where we created little key chains. Also on Wednesday afternoons we have a post-natal session, which is run by health visitors. We call it a baby-walking group but it's really a fitness group. The new mothers take their babies for walks through the park or along the footpaths in the afternoon and come back for a cup of coffee. This gives them the chance to chat, and the health visitors the opportunity to give a little advice, should it be needed.

We have the Residents Association meetings in our community room and local councillors hold their surgeries in there. We are just starting to negotiate for it to be used by the Citizens Advice Bureau and a couple of other agencies as there's no other suitable venue around here. It has been found that, with the changes in benefits, there's more and more need for a facility wherein confidential matters can be discussed with individuals in private. All this means the church can be used more for the community rather than just for religious services.

We've also brought our Christmas and summer fairs into the church rather than outside, which is a return to medieval practise. We have the fair going on in the nave, which is what would have happened some 800 years ago. The church would have been the only public building and everything happened there, such as the magistrates' court, and the stock sales in the churchyard. Any public meeting would have taken place in the church. We want the church to be used as much as possible, rather than for an hour on Wednesdays and Sundays.

We have to apply for funding to turn the church back into a community hall. The bishop talks about returning the church to what it was years ago. We're also dealing with population change in Ockendon with plans to build more housing as people continue to migrate from the East End.

Unfortunately we have to keep the church locked as the insurance premiums would be unaffordable if we were to keep it open.

Getting children into church is an interesting issue as it's rather difficult to get children to attend. We get large numbers of people on Remembrance Sunday here in St Nicholas, which includes Scouts' troupes and Guides, etc. We usually have about 500–600 people in the congregation and 150–200 of them will be children for that particular service. We have a dedicated children's service for Christmas at All Saints and that's very well attended. St Nicholas is the busier church at the moment, probably because it's the parish church and sits on the green. All Saints, which is in Foyle Drive, has the bigger Sunday congregation while St Nicholas is smaller, due probably to there being fewer people in the village.

In 1954 Sedgewick House in North Road was bought as the rectory but it was previously the dower house for South Ockendon Hall. The LCC demolished the old rectory in 1955 and built a housing estate on the site of the house and glebe.

Food banks are centred across Thurrock and we have one at All Saints, although we are all partner churches. The food is collected or bought from donations given to churches, community services etc. It's taken to the warehouse, which happens to be in South Ockendon, at the back of Belhus Park. There it's made up into boxes and taken to the distribution centres where

Christ in Glory, stained-glass window in St Nicholas church, in memory of the Cast family. (Courtesy of Benjamin Finn, St Peters Glasswork)

it becomes food parcels for say, single folk, couples and families in need. Then there are voucher centres at places like the Citizens Advice Bureau, some parts of social services, and some schools are also involved. They can be obtained at various places, and even some GPs have joined the scheme.

Vouchers are given on an emergency-only basis with just three vouchers given in succession, but people are also given access to other services. Should somebody say their benefits have ceased, for example, they are given advice as to what to do next. With the downturn in the economy we are seeing a lot of debt and people who have been working and running their own lives are now in dire straits. Their lives have come down like a pack of cards, so they need help to manage their debts and to feed their families. We hope that, by the time they've received three vouchers, they've approached the right people and are being given help. We mustn't build a dependence, and are not a supplement to social services but are there in cases of immediate need.

The voucher givers are not the same as the distribution centres. We've recently had collections for food in Tesco's and Morrison's, where we stood outside the supermarket with a big box and gave shoppers a leaflet as they went into the stores. We do about three or four collections a year, requesting items such as baby milk, packets and tins of food, and ask shoppers to add the odd extra item to their baskets. We also ask that if there's an offer to buy one and get one free, they give the free one to us. People are incredibly generous and the last time we did a collection at Asda in Tilbury we collected about a ton and a half of food. People donate because it's tangible and they can see what's happening. We will shortly have distribution centres in all four of our churches. They are only open for a few hours each week but we'll be covered for people in need throughout the parish.

Father Peter Rabin

Altar from the Hospital

The church at the South Ockendon Hospital was dedicated to Christ the Healer. When it closed they had to dispose of its contents so they asked local churches and groups to take anything they needed. I think the stained glass was sent to the repository at Ely and, as St Nicholas is the parish church, we were allowed to take the beautifully carved oak altar plus some other small items. We also took the memorial book.

When the hospital closed, the chaplain – Edmund Lever – who lived in Pear Tree Close, came to St Nicholas and acted as an honorary curate and generally helped us out. When he died he left some money to the church, so we used it to get the altar back into good condition. It had been used at the hospital for fourteen years to celebrate communion etc., so the Revd Lever did a lot of good work there. The top was suffering very badly from water damage and one of the upright pieces on the 'X' at the front was broken off so we had it repaired and had the top repolished. The Chi-Rho symbol – ☧ – on the front of the altar is commonly used to represent the name of Christ.

We were during an interregnum at the time, so I was heavily involved with the administration of the church, and the PCC (Parochial Church Council) decided it was a good use for the money Revd Lever left to us.

The stained-glass window at the side of the church was bought to commemorate the Cast family, who were bakers in South Ockendon. The previous window had been blown out when a bomb fell during the war and Roy Cast had always wanted it replaced. When he died, he left us some money, so we had the new one, which depicts Christ in Glory, specially designed for us.

The original church was built in the eleventh century with the tower being built first and, of course, various bits and pieces added, as is quite normal.

Altar at St Nicholas church.

It's unusual for a church to have a round tower in these parts, although they're quite common in Norfolk. There are only about seven in Essex and it's worthy of note that our church is the nearest to London that has such a tower.

The Lady Chapel was originally the Saltonstall Chapel. In 1928 the organ was moved into the priests' vestry as it was previously sited in the chapel and completely hid the beautiful Saltonstall wall monument. It's said the reason Sir Richard Saltonstall was knighted is that he paid for a number of the ships sent to fight the Spanish Armada. He was quite wealthy, owning lots of land in this area, and was elected Lord Mayor of London in 1597.

There was much renovation to the church by Richard Benyon. The acoustics are said to be very good so we're able to hold concerts and other musical events here.

As a lay reader, which is a voluntary role, I can conduct funerals but not any sacramental service, for example weddings and baptisms. I've been in this role for twenty-three years and my time is mostly taken up with visiting and generally anything that crops up. I also run Age Concern Thurrock, am involved with Citizens Advice Bureau, South Ockendon Community Forum, and all sorts of groups.

In 1988 we had a big festival in South Ockendon to observe the 400th anniversary of the defeat of the Spanish Armada, with everybody dressed in Tudor costume – we held a big market on The Green.

Thurrock did a re-enactment to celebrate Queen Elizabeth's speech to the troops at Tilbury, with the actress, Kate O'Mara, playing the part of Queen Elizabeth I. Our vicar at the time (Fr Harry Black) played the part of the vicar who met her as she stepped off the boat at Tilbury.

Glynis Pettit

Thurrock Garden Centre

My grandfather, Woodward Edwin Walsham, purchased part of Benton Farm, South Ockendon, after the Second World War. He rented the forty-six acres to Parrish & Sons of Ponds Farm, Aveley who continued farming the land until 1959.

My grandfather and father both owned a building company called W.E. Walsham Ltd, and my grandfather, Woody Walsham, was a good friend of Mr Claude Mead who lived at Harwood Hall, Upminster. Mr Mead already owned land at the back of our site, and once planning permission was granted to Harwood Hall Estates, they began to dig for sand and ballast in 1959.

Between 1959 and 1969, a minimum of 20,000 cubic yards of minerals were extracted annually. The area was excavated down to about eighteen feet, followed by the Greater London Council filling the excavation to within three feet of the surface with London rubbish. The site was finally capped in 1970 with topsoil.

With the area at South Ockendon levelled off and restored, I considered opening a garden centre on the remaining thirty-seven acres. I knew Mr Ted Smith, who owned the Orchard Garden Centre in Grays, and spoke to him about my idea. I also got in touch with a professional horticulturalist and asked his advice about the viability of my plans. He agreed that the site would be ideal but it was within the green belt. We did, however, manage to obtain planning permission because the councillors thought the project would be good for South Ockendon. The garden centre was built during 1978 and started trading in 1979 as South Ockendon Garden Centre. In the November, three months after we commenced trading, we had an official opening by the well-known gardening broadcaster, the late Percy Thrower, and the mayor, Councillor Arthur Barnes. As I was still involved in the building industry, I brought in a manager, Mr Ian Pate, and his wife Mary. In 1996 we changed the name to Thurrock Garden Centre.

Later, we managed to obtain planning permission for three more greenhouses and the barn-style building on the front, although the council would not permit us to build sideways. Over a period of six years we planted twenty acres of woodland and this allowed the council to rethink their planning decision. Hopefully, over the next couple of years, we plan to expand further.

I gained my knowledge of plants and associated horticultural information over the last thirty-six years, but we run a business and, therefore, employ qualified staff with excellent knowledge, including the use of chemicals and fertilisers and associated gardening products. It also takes many seasons to gain this knowledge, but our staff has a great deal of experience and understanding of the general public's demands on gardening advice and techniques.

We travel around Britain and Europe to source our plants, and our products are purchased from suppliers and manufacturers from across the

November 1979: Percy Thrower at the official opening of South Ockendon Garden Centre.

world. Our Christmas range is sourced from Holland, as well as suppliers in the UK. Our special Christmas area is prepared for opening late September, although our planning and purchasing commences at the start of the New Year.

We have customers coming to visit us from a radius of over twenty miles, some becoming regular returnees and very familiar faces to our staff. Our own longest-serving employee has been with the company for twenty-five years. We remain a family-run business, with three daughters working at the Centre and a son-in-law who is the managing director.

To date we have added various related departments and employ approximately forty staff. The restaurant is run in-house by our manageress and her staff. The aquatic area is managed by outside specialists and their staff.

John Walsham

South Ockendon Hospital

I had several jobs when I left school as I was biding my time until I could apply to join the Royal Navy when I became eighteen. I'd been working on the river and was made redundant so my father suggested I train to be a nurse at what was then known as The Colony and later became the South Ockendon Hospital.

I was reluctant to do this in case my pals thought I was a 'sissy', so tried for the position of orderly and eventually began working as a nursing assistant for six months. However, I began to enjoy looking after the patients and the general atmosphere that prevailed throughout the whole complex, so – encouraged by some of my colleagues – when I became eighteen that March, I applied to become a student nurse at South Ockendon Hospital. I started my three-year training course in June 1962 and in 1965 became a Registered Nurse for the Mentally Handicapped. Later on, in 1969, I went away to Oldchurch Hospital and did my training as a state registered nurse, so I have two qualifications. I was seconded to Oldchurch to do my SRN but in order to keep my salary I had to go back to work at South Ockendon for eighteen months.

Once I got into nursing I found it very interesting as to how people become mentally ill, i.e. by genetic mutation or arrested development of the brain – there are many reasons why. Then there's the non-specific – in other words it's not known why some people are born with psychiatric conditions. There are always unanswered questions.

Denis Powell being presented with his diploma and hospital badge after his third-year examination results, 1965.

The real point of what South Ockendon Hospital provided was shelter and treatment for the mentally disabled. I was in charge of about eight different wards over the thirty years and at one point headed the male nursing staff of the Gloucester Clinic, which was officially known as the Gloucester Medical Centre. The ward was named after the Duchess of Gloucester, who'd laid the foundation stone on a prior visit. It catered for people with physical ailments as well as mental disability and had its own operating theatre, X-ray department, dentistry and pathology department, etc. Bill Berry was a technician where they used to do screening for various types of mental handicap – some people had both physical and mental disabilities. It was also a research facility for people with chromosome abnormalities etc.

The wards were graded to suit the needs of the individual person and some had to be locked in for their own and other patients' safety.

The residents were encouraged to work when able to do so. Some were involved on Mollands Farm doing agricultural work, and helping with the pigs and chickens etc., with much of the produce being supplied to the hospital. There was patient activity for five days a week and some people did various jobs in the industrial unit, and all that worked were paid for their services.

Occupational therapy also took place, with the patients involved in various activities, such as knitting, sewing and producing numerous things, some of which were for sale. They also had their own evening clubs, which included a disco night and a cinema club.

As more money was provided by the authorities we were able to do more, and obtain more equipment. Fund raising was very intense and I think people from outside the hospital didn't realise how well looked after the residents were. I know there have been criticisms, and in any profession you get one or two who are not suited to the job, but there was much good work done in South Ockendon Hospital. It was home to some people for forty or fifty years and the staff worked with antiquated equipment and facilities.

We had small babies who had various ailments and most wards had a treatment room to deal with cuts and other minor injuries. An injury would have to be serious for the patient to go to an outside hospital.

A matron was in charge of the hospital and there would be a chief male nurse. Male staff only worked on male wards and female staff with females, except for children. When matron was on duty she was very strict.

We had a school for our own residents, but we also had a school in the grounds called Millards for children who came in daily from outside the hospital who needed extra help with their learning.

Lots of local people were employed by the hospital, which at its peak housed over 1,000 patients. Originally we came under the jurisdiction of the Leytonstone

House Hospital which was our headquarters, and then we were administered by the North East Metropolitan Regional Health Authority and later were transferred to the Basildon and Thurrock Health Authority.

Our aim was to try to get people to lead as normal a life as possible within the confines of the hospital. When I first went into the South Ockendon Hospital, I found it was a community within a community. We had sports facilities such as our own football pitch, tennis courts and a cricket square, all of which were shared by residents and staff. We even had our own swimming pool and, with all this at our disposal, we had an annual sports day where staff vied with residents.

Even shoe repairs were done on the site, since Willie Webb was a qualified cobbler as well as being a charge nurse.

Working within a community dedicated to the well-being of the patients made for, as near as possible, a contented atmosphere where the staff made friends and were able to maintain a social life, despite the long working hours.

I headed several wards during my tenure and found myself in charge when I was quite young; I found it difficult at times, particularly when dealing with older people. They'd been there for years and had lots of experience, so it was awkward when I had to tell them what to do. We had to manage diet, epilepsy, etc. with some patients needing to be fed and the older people shaved. They'd have to be escorted to school and their different therapies.

I met my wife while working at the hospital and we lived in a house belonging to the hospital in Mollands Lane. All the gardens of the houses owned by the hospital were beautifully kept.

We had boys of various ages on Pine Ward, where I worked for a long time. Some would go to school or occupational therapy, so there was a very positive side to most of what we did. There were wonderful parents who came in to help. One lady had two boys in there and she came in to sew on buttons and generally help out with patching things up. She'd sort through the boys' clothing to see what needed mending etc.

Later on we started buying our own electric irons so the boys always looked nice, then other wards began to raise their own money. Staff would bring things in and there was a very good Friends' Association which provided things, such as televisions and stereos.

We had a pet magpie on Pines we called Maggie. One cold morning in March we heard a tapping noise and one of the domestics shouted to me that somebody was knocking on the window. It was winter and early in the morning, so quite dark. I went outside and called out, and to my surprise, a large bird jumped on to my hand. I brought it into the kitchen and gave it some hot milk but when I took it outside to let it go, it circled the building then came back. It seemed to attach

Denis Powell with 'Maggie' the magpie.

itself to me as it would come through my office window and sit on my desk – and if a doctor came in, it would squawk him away. Eventually he made a nest in a grille in the wall and stayed for a couple of years. He'd take peanuts if we had them and the boys used to feed him. I'm afraid Maggie met a sad end as he got caught in a window as it was being closed by one of the boys.

We'd had our own Scouts, Guides and Wolf Cub troops, with people from the home chosen as pack leaders.

In the '60s we'd take some of the low-dependency patients for a holiday at Ramsay Lodge in Dovercourt. It was a big rambling mansion with orchards, and chickens running around the gardens. The people loved it there and particularly enjoyed the home cooking. By the '80s holidaying overseas became popular, so we'd take small numbers of our residents abroad, with probably a ratio of four residents to three staff.

There was a recreation hall within the hospital where we had weekly film shows and people from all around the area came to the Saturday night dances. They'd bring their friends and enjoy practising the latest dances on the sprung floor. Often the proceeds had gone into war effort funds, but that was before my time. The recreation hall, which is now available for private hire, still stands on the site which was developed into private housing known as Brandon Groves.

I left three years before the hospital closure, as they'd started reducing staff and there wasn't a job available that I thought suitable for my qualifications. They'd begun moving residents into units in the community and were downgrading staff,

Community Hall, Brandon Groves.

so what was on offer would have affected my pension. They were housekeeper jobs where I'd have been responsible not only for the community home but for the gardens, etc. and the situation didn't appeal to me.

Most of the former residents, who are still living, are in community homes now and a lot of the residents who weren't from the vicinity went back to the areas which were responsible for them. They're not called residents any more but are known as service users.

At this point I decided to train once again, this time in chiropody. I'd always been interested in foot ailments, so took the two-year course. Once qualified, I worked as a visiting chiropodist and found myself being called back to the community homes to tend to the feet of my former patients. When practising as a chiropodist it's always necessary to take refresher courses to keep abreast with new procedures etc. and it was when another was due that I decided it was time to give it up. I finally retired in 2008.

Denis Powell

Pigs and Chickens

The hospital in South Road was known as The Colony in my time and there were children in there who had disabilities. A lot of the patients worked in the factories all round Thurrock and I used to go there to play football with those inmates who were able. They had the Colony Farm in Mollands Lane and some of the people went down there to look after the pigs and chickens.

Eric Jiggens

Chicken Farm

Another uncle had eleven children and he worked in the South Ockendon Hospital over the road where he ran their chicken farm – in that way they were well supplied with meat and eggs etc. They didn't check on the eggs and, because chickens breed quickly, they didn't know how many they had so Uncle used to give spare eggs, and the odd chicken, to people when they were in need – he was a very thoughtful man.

The hospital held the most beautiful New Year's Eve ball where the doctors used to wear dress shirts and the nurses were all dressed up looking lovely – it was a wonderful evening. My air force crew used to ask for tickets and I'd bring them down from Cambridge, where we were stationed. When I worked for the speedway I used to bring that team to the ball as well.

Jim McGillivray

British Legion

I've belonged to the Manor Park branch of the British Legion for eighteen years, and go to meetings fortnightly. For seventeen years I've been a standard carrier for them and for the same length of time have been collecting money for the annual Poppy Appeal, which helps the British Legion look after the needs of all ex-servicemen. I stand, with others, at Liverpool Street station for the two weeks prior to Remembrance Sunday. The style of poppies sold varies throughout the world and in Scotland, for example, their poppies have no leaf. One of our members sends to North America for Canadian poppies and we provide these especially for Canadians working or living in London.

Nearly every platform at Liverpool Street will have a collecting box and I normally sit at a table by the upstairs entrance near McDonald's. We have just the collection tin and a box of poppies on the table. We have to be watchful as there could be undesirables lurking round the station, but there's a massive police presence. Both British Rail police and City of London police keep an eye on us, as we're quite vulnerable to those who'd steal the money.

Ted Barton (forefront) with colleagues, 'forming up' for a British Legion parade.

Since I need to be present at a parade at St Paul's within this time, it makes for a busy two weeks. There are lots of us collecting at Liverpool Street, with nearly every platform having a collecting box, and there'll be other sites too. The generosity of the public is unbelievable. Hence, last year our branch alone collected £87,000. We're rarely given less than £1 for a poppy and quite often somebody will donate a £20 note. Help for Heroes is a charity that does a lot for our chaps who come home from Afghanistan etc., but the British Legion looks after them too.

Ted Barton

Nine

REFLECTIONS

Five Pubs

There were five pubs in Ockendon, because it was on the main road which led from Brentwood to Purfleet.

Peter Coe

Easter

As Easter came round, Mr Abraham, the baker from Upminster, used to go round the streets selling hot cross buns from a board he carried on his head. He rang his bell as he made his way through the village.

John Litton

Pamela Russell

I knew Champion Russell's daughter, Pamela, and I think she married an American so left the country. Later in life my parents downsized and moved to a bungalow in Fen Lane. It was one of two in Fen Lane which were funded by the Russell family and known as the memorial bungalows. The Russells left some money to the North Ockendon community and it was a coincidence that Dad helped to build the bungalows.

Pam Bonnett

So Glad to be Home

When my husband eventually came home from the war he said he'd never leave North Ockendon again and he mostly stuck to his word, although we did manage to get him away for one or two holidays later on.

Evelyn Cressey

V2 Rocket Site

In a field on the left of Fen Lane, before you reach the cottages, you can still see the site where a V2 rocket fell. It is now a circle of trees/bushes, in the centre of which is a pond.

Geoff Jones

Stubbers

When I was about ten, I delivered the post and newspapers to Champion Russell of Stubbers and his cook would make me a little breakfast. In those days we all worked from when we were young. They had beautiful gardens in Stubbers and Miss Russell, the daughter, was a wonderful gardener who lectured on plants etc. in the schools. When the family gave Stubbers up she went to live at Warley and they turned Stubbers into a sports centre.

Peter Coe

Daffodils

I have a lovely memory of Stubbers. Each spring, I think on the Saturday, we'd go there with the Sunday school to pick flowers. There were rows of daffodils at the back of the house and we'd pick them, then bunch them up to give to our mothers in church on Mothering Sunday.

Pam Bonnett

Rabbiting

We used to go rabbiting in the dark, because there were lots of them on the cricket pitch. Dad didn't earn a lot, so in those days we always had a big cooking pot with a couple of rabbits in it because we caught rabbits and kept chickens. I used to keep ferrets, so we'd go ferreting.

Vic Rampling

The Red Lion

Buses only ran on the hour, with the last one going through North Ockendon at half-past eight in the evening, so we all had to cycle.

There'd been an old coaching inn on the corner called the Red Lion – it was no longer operating as a pub but used as a cafe. Mrs Pook had the little sweet shop next door.

John Litton

Old White Horse

A Mrs Arbory was in the Old White Horse when I came here – it was just an ale house then.

Evelyn Cressey

The Old White Horse ale house *c.* 1900s.

Blacksmith

Mr Cressey, the blacksmith, used to allow us to pump up his bellows in the forge.

When we first came to North Ockendon we lived in Ivy Dene Cottage, before we moved to Clay Tye Cottage.

Gwen Bishop

Firewood

My uncle used to chop wood during the week and go round to the houses with a horse and cart selling firewood at the weekend, as everybody cooked on a stove in those days.

Jim McGillivray

Casts

There was another general shop in South Ockendon owned by Casts – related to Casts the bakers. The latter lived in The Bakery by the corner of Fen Lane, but the bread was baked in South Ockendon and delivered to North Ockendon for them to sell in the shop.

Peter Coe

Also from The History Press

ESSEX

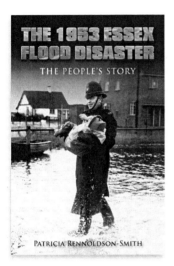

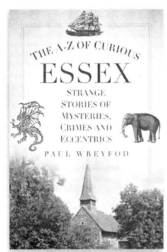

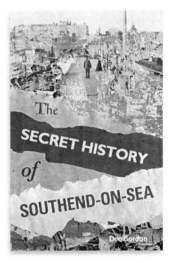

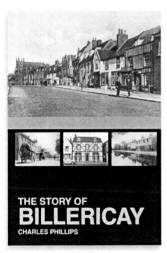

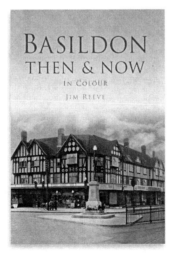

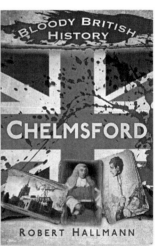

Also from The History Press

BACK TO SCHOOL

Also from The History Press

GREAT WAR BRITAIN

Great War Britain is a unique new local series to mark the centenary of the Great War. In partnership with archives and museums across Great Britain, the series provides an evocative portrayal of life during this 'war to end all wars'. In a scrapbook style, and beautifully illustrated, it includes features such as personal memoirs, letters home, diary extracts, newspaper reports, photographs, postcards and other local WWI ephemera.

Lightning Source UK Ltd.
Milton Keynes UK
UKOW04f2350110414

229838UK00005B/8/P